Therapeutic Connectedness

The Central Importance of the Unique and New Relationship

**Edited by
M. Sagman
Kayatekin**

Therapeutic Connectedness

The Central Importance of the Unique and New Relationship

Edited by M. Sagman Kayatekin

IPBOOKS.net

International Psychoanalytic Books (IPBooks)
New York • www.IPBooks.net

International Psychoanalytic Books (IPBooks), Queens, NY

Online at: www.IPBooks.net

Cover and interior book design by Kathy Kovacic, Blackthorn Studio

ISBN: 978-1-956864-97-7

Therapeutic Connectedness: The Central Importance of the Unique and New Relationship

Edited by M. Sagman Kayatekin

From the Desk of the Editor-in-Chief

M. Sagman Kayatekin

The current issue you are holding is the first one I edited in my new role as the Editor in Chief of the International Journal of Controversial Discussions. I am humbled by and enjoying the honor of following Arnold Richards as the new Editor-in-Chief. Arnie, a mentor and friend has been quite difficult to emulate and also a source of aspiration and inspiration for me for many years.

The defining aspect of the workings of the journal and its mission is well summarized by Arnie Richards in our webpage:

"The IJCD model of peer review is that papers that are well written and well-reasoned are published and responded to publicly by a discussant with similar interests. The author is then given the opportunity to respond. The IJCD does not have any theoretical or ideological bias and will cast a wide net including contributors from many disciplines and many geographical locations. It will consider a broad array of subjects of interest to mental health professionals. The journal is a work in progress, and we welcome input from the larger mental health community."

We are living in an era of dramatic change, where dialogue in developing new ideas and reviewing old ideas is becoming more obviously important to our common intellectual consciousness. In contrast to our earlier formulations of ideas developing in individual isolation, we now understand that humans do indeed develop ideas as a part of ongoing, ever expanding and deepening conversation within groups, with others. One may say the IJCD will follow the lead of this newly understood aspect of the creativity of human mind, the Hegelian "Seele".

In sum, the philosophy of the journal is well coded in its name—International Journal of Controversial Discussions. We hope to develop a forum where creative controversy leads to finding new ideas. And we will try our best to avoid endless ruminative antagonisms.

This issue will focus on the recent book of Jane S. Hall, "The Power of Connection" published by International Psychoanalytic Books (IPBooks) New York 2022 (https://ipbooks.net)

Jane Hall with her writing fits this philosophy wonderfully. In a plain language, she tells the stories of an alive person, herself, in the act of therapeutic love and thinking about others, with others. Her evocativeness allows one to have a lively dialogue with a text that is quite open about the workings of her mind, her weaknesses, strengths and endless curiosity about fellow humans. In this issue, we will read the responses to her stories, thoughts and work by various psychoanalytic clinicians and scholars. I hope you will enjoy the dialogues in the following narratives as much as I did.

With respectful and warm regards to our readers.

M. Sagman Kayatekin

"Introduction and Philosophy"

Jane Hall

The analyst's feeling of certainty is often tied to the idea that there exists a proper "analytic technique" derived from ideas passed down from one generation of analysts to the next (which may be codified by particular "schools" of analytic thinking). By contrast, think of "analytic style" as one's own personal creation that is loosely based on existing principles of analytic practice, but more importantly is a living process that has its origins in the personality and experience of the analyst.

–Ogden (2007)

Too many writers cannot come to terms with the ways in which the past, like the future, is dark. There is so much we don't know, and to write truthfully about a life, your own or your mother's, or a celebrated figure's, an event, a crisis, another culture is to engage repeatedly with those patches of darkness, those nights of history, those places of unknowing. They tell us that there are limits to knowledge, that there are essential mysteries, starting with the notion that we know just what someone thought or felt in the absence of exact information.

–Rebecca Solnit (2014)

You know I went to school
And I'm nobody's fool
That is to say until I met you!
I know a little bit about a lot o' things
But I don't know enough about you

–Peggy Lee (1946)

3

What follows is offered with humility during a worrisome time—a time with strains of Covid haunting the world, a time of global warming with its tragic effects, a time of fighting prejudice, of increasing gun violence, and a time of serious division in America that threatens democracy. How we react, adjust, protest, and survive depends a lot on how we use our energy effectively. Mental health must be a priority.

This collection is for anyone who is curious about how one psychoanalyst's thoughts have evolved after five decades in the field. Thanks to my own meandering journeys, my own on-going self-analysis, and thanks to my patients, to those I supervise and teach, and to my colleagues, I feel freer and more curious every day, and the design of this book reflects that. Longer essays, shorter riffs and even a poem will hopefully provide food for thought. After all these years I am increasingly interested in how the brain and the mind are related and how depth therapy figures in. I am most interested in how a dyad connects and what that connection can accomplish.

I must say up front that some of these ideas will seem old hat to many, and to some they will sound un-psychoanalytic, so my hope is for open-minded consideration. I respect many theories of technique because we are all unique and because we are exploring unchartered territory with each patient. My slant is just that: a slant. It is a perspective that I offer based on my work with patients, many of whom have experienced degrees of childhood strain trauma that interfered with optimal development. It is a perspective that is influenced by a basic knowledge about neural pathways in the brain; how the stress hormone cortisol, and the love hormone oxytocin affect the brain's development (Doidge, 2007); and by new research findings about development (Knight, 2021).

I have always believed that the emergence of negative transference and the rage upon which it is based needs expression, but the question is: how much and for how long. How the dyad deals with it, and what they learn from its expression, is one of the most important questions in our work because an ongoing expression of primitive rage can wear both parties down and may engrave an original trauma more deeply in the brain's neural pathways. Of course, the answers depend on the unique patient's history, but when development has been derailed, and I believe this happens more often than we recognize or realize, we must find ways to get it back on track. This includes learning about our earliest days which is sometimes possible but most times not, along with our history of relationships. Think in terms of knitting a sweater. Dropped stitches in the beginning can be easily overlooked when the sweater is finished unless you look carefully. But will the sweater hold its shape over time? Unfinished or incomplete developmental tasks can be hard to spot in the adult patient, especially in the beginning stages of analytic treatment, but when impasse threatens or progress is stalled due to a patient's difficulty with reality, I have found that solid enough differentiation between self and object and incomplete separation and individuation need attention. So many things too numerous to list, including genetic disposition, how mother and baby match, illness, and early loss to name just a few, impinge upon how the child takes in and processes its surrounds. These things are what make us unique.

With this in mind, I am suggesting a level playing field with two people working together, where the analyst shares her strength with her partner until her partner feels increasingly stronger. In other words, I am considering how we redress the damage done by varieties of trauma which affect, to varying degrees, the tasks of differentiation between self and object, the separation-individuation process, and the formation of a self. I think that many patients reach impasses if this is overlooked. We are also faced with the serious dissociation that occurs in patients subjected to severe, ongoing trauma. Purcell (2019) informs us in his moving paper that with "unrepresented experience–something different is needed at the level of "technique": a technical attitude—one of doing things to our patients—must largely be replaced by a way of being with our patients… being with his analysand in non-meaning as well as in symbolic communication. In being the analyst for traumatized people, technical rules and maneuvers must give way to improvisation and creativity, integral elements of an artistry that must find its place in the analyst's attitude."

My imaginary reader shares with me the insatiable wish to understand the mysteries of why we are who we are. Having reached a certain age I realize that the more I see and the more I learn, the more I recognize how much more there is to discover. I have gained an increasing appreciation of how very complicated the human mind and brain are, and I am in awe of those who dedicate their time and energy to understanding how the mind interacts with the brain, how the outside affects the inside, and how epigenetic change occurs. Psychoanalysis offers the most thorough approach to solving such mysteries, especially when scientific research is acknowledged. Cultivating and keeping an open mind makes almost everything seem possible.

These heretofore unpublished essays and riffs were written over the past ten plus years, some quite recently, and are now the chapters of this book. My focus is on how the connection between two people, known as the dyad, encourages the growth that leads to change. Even our most challenging patients hopefully come to know on some level when someone is listening without criticism. This book is a sequel to *Deepening the Treatment*, and the reader will see that my philosophy has shifted from a more classical view of our work to what I consider a more contemporary one that takes into consideration research in neuroscience, affects, and child development.

How two strangers connect, and the importance of that connection is the underlying theme of this book. Conversation connects us, whether in person, on Zoom-like platforms, via email or snail mail, or over the telephone. I think that all the words we use, even in one session or over the entire course of treatment, serve as the glue that bind the dyad together. And sometimes I think that if our hearts are in the right place, it matters not so much what we say to each other but how we say it. Angry words, loving words, fancy words, empty words, lack of words are important yet when all is said and done, neither party in the dyad remembers much of what was said when treatment has ended. What is remembered are the feelings beneath the words and the spontaneous moments of laughter, tears, and of feeling genuinely caring, cared about, and accepted.

About the couch: During analysis there are times when reading a person's facial expression is beneficial for both parties in the dyad. This is particularly important for the patient with an avoidant attachment style where the goal is connecting positively with a new object instead of reinforcing memories of the early, depriving and traumatic objects. When patients repeat the past in the transference instead of using it as a clue to the mystery, such repetition risks reinforcing the original trauma. As a new object relationship is formed by in depth, libidinal connection with the analyst over time, the brain's circuitry changes. The phrase 'use it or lose it' applies here so if you had a bad object relationship with a parent, and then you develop a better one with a new object, the fact that you have a trace of the old one doesn't mean you have to use it (Doidge, 2007).

Our first conversations in life take the form of the cooing and crying of infancy and the way they are responded to. These earliest connections play a major part in determining the bond we form with our mothers/caretakers and serve as a major template for future relationships. There is solid evidence that human beings are inextricably intertwined with one another from the earliest moments of infancy. At birth, the infant appears hard-wired to seek human interaction. Along with words, conversation includes how we communicate with our eyes, our posture, odor, style, our facial expressions, silences, the way we listen, and especially our unconscious vibes. In psychoanalysis the conversation goes on consistently over time in a safe place with a non-judgmental, trustworthy other.

Analysis involves a certain amount of regression, so the couch is helpful for those who have frequent enough sessions. But at times it is useful to read a person's facial expression, particularly with the deprived adult with an avoidant attachment style. I like the idea of a swivel reclining chair for the patient who can then have a choice.

One of the most important things I have learned is that those who have grown up with unavailable, narcissistic, or abusive parents or caretakers have trouble giving and receiving love as adults. We get used to our earliest diets and have great difficulty in digesting new food. We seek out the same restaurants because the food is familiar and familiarity means safety, even when painful. We choose partners who echo the past because feeling safe is a basic need. I see no harm in mentioning this tendency to a patient at an appropriate time.

It is my hope that with these chapters I succeed in connecting with you, the reader, as I talk about my philosophy of clinical work, my experiences with patients, and what I have learned as a clinician, consultant, and teacher.

This collection is meant not only for depth psychotherapists, but also for anyone interested in psychoanalytic ideas. My pronouns switch at random for the sake of brevity and out of respect for gender preferences. I use the word 'patient' out of habit. (A patient is any recipient of health care services that are performed by healthcare professionals.) I would prefer 'learner' or 'adventurer' or 'partner in solving mysteries' but I fear this would sound too futuristic. 'Co-traveler' would be good too because I see psychoanalytic work as a journey taken by two, a meandering journey (Chapter Three).

Why another book? The field is crowded with interesting, scholarly, and useful literature and I'm sure that just about everything has been said, one way or another. Many psychoanalysts are excellent writers who have even contributed fiction, memoir, and poetry. Ted Jacobs, Tom Ogden, Christopher Bollas, Arlene Heyman, Sandra Beuchler,

Eugene Mahon, and Kerry Malawista come immediately to mind. Many erudite authors are sometimes more difficult to read but often well worth the effort. My style/voice is direct— no vibrato, just plain and simple. Speaking of voices, I use jazz music in Chapter Ten, On Listening, to encourage the idea of creating something new.

Hopefully, my slant, that has been developing over all these years will be of use. Also, I have been working on these essays and riffs for a long time with the hope that someone will get something from them. The song *"T'ain't What You Do, It's the Way That You Do It"* comes to mind because our voices make us unique. One more reason: psychoanalytic observations and theories have gained sophistication over the years and so have psychoanalytic clinicians. Our methods are now making use of the impressive research in child development and in neuroscience. I want to encourage therapists to fight the lure of *received wisdom* and to allow new findings to stretch their minds.

"...you work to turn the ghosts that haunt you into ancestors who accompany you. That takes hard work and a lot of love, but it is the way we lessen the burdens our children have to carry...I work to be an ancestor" said Bruce Springsteen in *Born to Run.* Hans Loewald also spoke of turning ghosts into ancestors. In fact, isn't that what all we clinicians do? Ghost busting is our business.

Freud deserves our deepest respect and appreciation. He will always accompany us but psychoanalytic work has advanced and branched out to serve all kinds of people as I'm sure he would have wanted it to. By the way, Freud was far more re-lational than many of his followers have acknowledged. He conducted a number of walking analyses, according to Peter Gay in *Freud: A Life for Our Time.* (Gay 1988). Besides his four hours walk with Gustav Mahler, Freud conducted his first training analysis on Max Eitingon in 1907 through a se-ries of evening walks. Eitingon went on to become president of the International Psychoanalytic Association and created a model of training still used today. I sometimes wonder whether some of our founding fathers and mothers analyzed their sadomasochistic tendencies with such short analyses; and how their influence affects us in today's analytic world.

Freud's phallocentric, oedipal focus has been challenged by Breger (2009), Barron (1991) Simon (1991), and Holtzman & Kulish (2000) among others. The research on attachment and the separation-individuation tasks of development featuring both the maternal and paternal influences has changed the phallocentric focus.

As I look at today's world with so many adamant believers in bizarre conspiracies, along with the rampant misogyny finally being brought to justice thanks to the "me too" movement, I believe that early childhood anxieties and the transmission of trauma play a large part. Paranoia can be seen as one result of early and ongoing anxiety. It has always been a part of society but social media fans its flames. With society's pressures increasing, many parents are unable to provide the safety and security that children need in order to differentiate and to individuate. Parents cannot help but pass on their own fears and anxiety to their children who often fail to develop a secure sense of self. This is not new, but the research is now available proving that children thrive under certain conditions. And even when parents are caring and available, things can go radically wrong due to certain social media platforms.

My ideas about leveling the playing field and distancing our techniques from the medical model harken back to when psychoanalysis came to America in 1911 as a medical sub-specialty. The analyst as a medical doctor, all too often took on the persona of a blank screen that was meant to help the patient develop a transference neurosis (an emotional relationship with the analyst based on childhood relationships). This has been referred to as classical or orthodox psychoanalysis. The results of a lawsuit claiming restraint of trade, and settled in 1989, changed the profession by allowing psychologists, social workers, and qualified others to join the ranks by studying at the American Psychoanalytic training institutes. However, their teachers were M.D.s whose model featured diagnosis, prognosis, and cure. This model heavily influenced the field in America. I join many who question seeing the analyst in the role of the physician administering a treatment based upon a judgment of psychopathology which determines analyzability. The infantilization of the patient (and of the student in training) has seriously harmed this field. Even the word 'training' instead of education illustrates a less than humanistic attitude. So-called 'lay analysts' were ignored by the medical establishment despite Freud's impassioned plea (1926). Theodore Reik, a non-M.D., began his own independent institute, the National Psychological Association for Psychoanalysis (https://en.wikipedia.org/wiki/National Psychological_Association_for_Psychoanalysis) dedicated to teaching non-physicians. Others soon followed suit.

The view I take is a continuation of Leo Stone's (1954) humanistic approach. I am most impressed by Sandor Ferenczi who envisioned the analysand as a co-participant in the dyad. I appreciate and support the emphasis on empathic reciprocity during the therapeutic encounter which is an important contribution from the evolution of the intersubjective/relational school of psychoanalysis. Both parties in the dyad must be free to share experiences when appropriate, in contrast to the abstinent/blank screen approach advocated by the orthodox analysts. I see the dyad as a partnership that leaves room for the evolving transferences to be understood and adjusted thus allowing for something new. Freud's followers in Berlin led by Max Eitingon did him a disservice by bringing an authoritarian approach to both students and patients.

I learned, practiced, and appreciate many ideas espoused by the classical model but differ with its *analyst as blank screen* approach because it deprives patients of forming a new human connection that I find indispensable to growth. The medical model initially practiced in America could not help but affect how the analyst and patient viewed each other and this patient/doctor image, understandable as it may be in other circumstances, is what I suggest needs adjusting. I propose in these essays and riffs a basic shift in the way many (not all) psychoanalysts still work with patients. The mindset of a doctor implies a top-down, authoritarian slant and our society bows to this approach. We want a doctor to cure us and here is where I offer a different point of view. The idea of working together to get development back on track is very different from a doctor curing a patient by interpreting her free associations. It is different because as patients resume development it is they who do what is necessary to move forward in life. I see the therapist as facilitating development. Along these lines I propose that explanation and conversation take the place of interpretation. Yes, the analyst shares what she hears but not as a pronouncement.

The shift that I envision suggests a level playing field where two people view problems together—as co-workers. This does not preclude transference explanations; we all see the present influenced by past experience. But both partners use their transference vision in the service of going beyond. This approach is especially applicable to those whose early years were unsteady and traumatic. What I am proposing is that both parties in the dyad discuss possible ways of understanding the clues presented by the patient, rather than setting up the analyst as the authoritative interpreter—the one with the answers. The attitude that includes discussion in and of itself builds the patient's ego or sense of agency. This idea will not be new to many depth therapists who have not undergone classical analytic training that focuses on analysis of defense.

I am not concerned here with talking about theories, such as Intersubjective or Self-psychology or the structural versus the topographic, and so forth, and I don't dwell on differentiating psychoanalysis and psychoanalytic psychotherapy, a topic that has plagued this field for too many years. Beneath the theories lay the therapist's stance. Does she see disease/illness/pathology, or does she think in terms of derailed development and once necessary adaptations that are no longer useful or necessary? How a clinician views a patient's difficulties is what I suggest needs serious rethinking. Instead of focusing on what's *wrong* exclusively, I suggest seeing what's right. We all adapt as best we can to the cards, we've been dealt in childhood so why call this pathology? Early adaptations have been lifesaving if you think about it—but like childhood shoes, we outgrow them. The right to have new shoes is what therapists hope to instill. Benevolent curiosity (Sharpe, 1930) is the bedrock of the method I am presenting. Her words:

> *"The urgency to reform, correct, or make different motivates the task of a reformer or educator, the urgency to cure motivates the physician, but free to range over every field of human experience and activity, free to recognize every unconscious impulse, with only one urgency, namely, a desire to know more, and still more. When we react to something that causes us to think 'I cannot understand how a person can think or behave like that' curiosity has ceased to be benevolent."*

Thanks to the research on child development (Knight, 2021; Tronick, 2011) and the discovery of the brain's plasticity, the psychoanalyst's palette is filled with more colors than our forefathers and mothers had available. I propose adding to or even replacing Freud's phallocentric, oedipal model with a developmental model, featuring the quality of the bond between the infant and its caretakers, the separation-individuation phase with its task of differentiating self from object, as central. To put it plainly: too many have not fully realized that there are 'others' who think differently and so are unable to respect diversity. I see the analytic goal as getting derailed development back on track. For those who find Mahler's model limited, I suggest Ed Tronick's (2001) Dyadic Expansion of Consciousness hypothesis. But both theories center on the child's early connection to the mothering figure. Thanks to Rona Knight's research we have learned that development continues throughout life and is not limited to specific ages.

My extensive experience with patients who suffered strain trauma in childhood has shaped many of the ideas in this book. Although I respect and consider the many theories available, I am committed to greeting each patient as unique. Our tendency to apply a diagnosis and then a theory to an individual limits what we see. The unique patient creates the theory (Nass, 1975).

Technique has changed gradually in that its elements, such as furniture and frequency, are no longer written in stone. But many training institutes guided by the Eitingon model still require these artifacts. Why do we cling to them? Yes, using the couch can be helpful but making its use a requirement is insensitive to the unique individual.

This book takes issue with the analyst as mostly silent interpreter of the patient's free associations. I picture two people facing the problems together as detectives solving mysteries? (See Lois in Chapter Three: Self-Murder.) This stance requires respect and benevolent curiosity. Over time the dyad develops a relationship that includes transference love, real love, hatred, and everything in between. Transferences serve as clues. When patients see the others in their lives only in terms of past relationships, their vision needs adjustment. The dyad works together to broaden their view. I must add that I respect the analyst's silence as well. Our patient's must have the opportunity to see where their minds go—so I hope for a flexible approach with the unique patient in mind. A rhythm evolves that accelerates at times and that slows at other times. No metronomes are required.

In essence, I propose that two people share the job of looking into how the past affects the present, with the resumption of development being the goal. The feelings and fantasies (conscious and unconscious) experienced by both parties are explored. One partner may hold the other's anxiety until it diminishes due to the connection that develops. Most of what goes on is unconscious and when enactments that are always happening become evident, the unconscious message is exposed. This exposure releases us from an action mode thus allowing insight. Tronick (1998) suggests that there are dyadic states of consciousness that develop between patient and therapist that he calls 'something more'—and that change is due to these new and unique dyadic states. Purcell (2019) speaks about "a way of being."

Anxiety diminishes when criticism is not involved. In Chapter Nine: "How Long," Lisa's constant tears in the beginning phase of analysis may have been expressing her fear of criticism. Love, not often enough mentioned in our literature, grows out of respect and serves to cushion the discomfort involved in negotiating separation and individuation. Benevolent curiosity is part of love.

We need the new discoveries about the brain and mind. Norman Doidge's message in *The Brain That Changes Itself,* is that during analytic work we choose different neural pathways when the old ones lead to trouble—a bold idea based on the evidence of the brain's plasticity. See Chapter One of his book where he describes the stroke victim's recovery and what the brain autopsy showed after a long and productive life.

I have seen classical analysis help some people, but a combination of methods can be useful depending on the unique dyad. The analyst must feel free to titrate the treatment with the unique patient in mind while still calling the treatment psychoanalysis if she so wishes. I believe many of us already feel this freedom, so this is meant for those who have felt intimidated by their 'training.' What I suggest is partially based on my own personal experiences, one with an authoritarian training analyst followed by a vastly different personal telephone analysis with a highly respected and revered analyst who refused the title on principle. These experiences helped shape the ideas in these essays.

My major focus is the therapist's slant, attitude, and manner—a manner that is based on respect, a special kind of love, and benevolent curiosity, all three allowing us to experience the patient as unique.

Short riffs and longer essays and even a poem (though by no means am I a poet) express some of what I've learned. Neither textbook nor memoir—I present my personal slant on the journey including what I've learned from my experience. While doing research I was floored by the richness of our literature. The plethora of books and articles about psychoanalytic work can only mean that we are forever searching for and sharing ideas. And why not? The human mind is extremely complex, as is the brain and its outposts. Both deserve all the attention we can muster. There is no one way of thinking that captures its mysteries which relates to my feelings about the disadvantages and harm involved in measurement. The way we use the new discoveries mentioned above surely matters just as much as the evidence itself. Ed Tronick and Marjorie Beeghly (2011) speak of an instinct or drive towards *making meaning* that we are all born with and this makes perfect sense to me. There is so much to learn and see and experience. And sometimes, depending on how we use it, all our knowledge can actually impede us and even obscure what our partner is telling us.

Our most famous fictional detective, Sherlock Holmes, says as much in this story:

> *Holmes and Watson are on a camping trip. In the middle of the night Holmes wakes up and gives Dr. Watson a nudge. "Watson" he says, "look up...and tell me what you see." "I see millions of stars, Holmes," says Watson. "And what do you conclude from that, Watson?" Watson thinks for a moment. "Well," he says, "astronomically, it tells me that there are millions of galaxies and potentially billions of planets. Astrologically, I observe that Saturn is in Leo. Horologically, I deduce that the time is approximately a quarter past three. Meteorologically, I suspect that we will have a beautiful day tomorrow. Theologically, I see that God is all-powerful, and we*

are small and insignificant. Uh, what does it tell you, Holmes?" "Watson, you idiot! Someone has stolen our tent!"

A recent reading in Jack Pankseep's (2005) work on affects, coupled with understanding more about the intersubjective/ relational approach so well-articulated by Phillip Bromberg, Lew Aron, Stephen Mitchell, Donnel Stern, Jim Fosshage, and so many others, and recognizing the plasticity of the brain have shifted my thinking to a broader comprehension of how we relate to each other and to our patients. Heart to heart communication is what matters most, and it often takes place without words. I repeat, more goes on unconsciously than we can ever know. This is why the therapist's hope is important. Our patient's pick it up subliminally.

I have always shied away from diagnostic categories because I fear boxing people in. They provide some advantages, as Nancy McWilliams (2011) has beautifully shown us, but for many therapists these categories can stand in the way of hope. Nancy says:

> *"Once one has learned to see clinical patterns that have been observed for decades, one can throw away the book and savor individual uniqueness."*

However, my concern is that such patterns can affect what we see and experience. I worry that we are too comfortable experiencing a unique individual as being just another hysteric or borderline or obsessive compulsive described in the DSMs. This may obscure other features and patterns that make discovery of the uniqueness of each individual quite difficult if not impossible. If Copernicus had stayed with the received wisdom that the earth and not the sun was the center of our universe, science would not have advanced. *Received wisdom* can be wrong! My point is that the way people have seen things for decades, directs and clouds our vision. Of course, I realize that what we have learned will always influence us, but my plea is to be aware of the tendency to categorize, and to replace that tendency by cultivating an open mind. Hearing a person as a unique individual must come first. If we need a frame of reference how about this: the past determines the present and what cannot be articulated will be enacted or acted out. There is a natural course of development and when it has been compromised it is the dyad's job to clear the way for its resumption. Patients who are uncooperative have reasons!

I have not seen evidence that convinces me of the categories that DSM has devised even though they are compelling, and I *have* seen evidence that these categories tend to narrow our thinking, influence our perception, and leave us spinning our wheels. But most importantly, a label can obscure the uniqueness of each individual patient. So, although there is comfort in categories when used as shorthand, or for insurance companies, I fear that the patient and the therapist may get lost in the label. Boxes are like fences to me and a favorite song of mine is *Don't Fence Me In.* I think in terms of development, so separation-individuation and its sub-phases, along with object constancy, and differentiation, are helpful concepts. Did someone get stuck along the way, and if they did, how can they get back on track, I wonder? I use the word "wonder" a lot because it leaves the door open for new ideas and because I hope my co-traveler will wonder too. The arrogance of certainty cuts off so many options.

Phillip Bromberg's (1996) work with self-states makes great sense to me as does a favorite book by a non-analyst psychologist *Stranger in the Mirror: the scientific search of the self,* by Robert V. Levine (2017). Both authors write from different backgrounds but come to similar conclusions: we have many self-states that are not problematic. One is not using the same self-state when facing an emergency as when learning a subject in school or when making love. In fact, what we deem pathology was once adaptive. If we see the adaptive aspects of defensive character structure, our ability to relate to our patients is enhanced. People often forget to think "What's right with you?" Seeing the glass half full helps me. I have said to a patient something like: *"Hiding from the truth (avoidance or denial) was helpful when you were a child but now it holds you back. It's like trying to walk in shoes you have outgrown. They helped then but now they pinch making it hard to move ahead."*

But you will say, what about the truly impossible patient, the patient who is hostile to the whole idea of therapy. Chapter One, Let's Fall in Love, discusses this dilemma. Bottom line, it is up to the therapist to find creative ways to respond. And sometimes treatment just doesn't get to first base. We do strike out. We are human.

Therapists, like their patients, like to feel safe, and because the familiar is safe, we often cling to it. What we learn in the psychoanalytic institute is difficult to forget. It took me many years to move beyond what I learned in the 1970s and 1980s. I question the set-up of our learning institutes. Just as each patient is unique, so is each student and I hope that can be taken into account. Tailoring our knowledge to the individual is an art that must be nurtured. Each dyad creates something unique. So, when I said in the beginning of this introduction that nothing is new, I also think everything is new when you expand your vision. I recently discovered David Eagleman, and I highly recommend his podcast Inner Cosmos, his TED Talks and books.

Readers who are dissatisfied, in pain, or curious about psychoanalytic work may be inspired to take a journey inward with an experienced companion. I know of no other journey that is more fulfilling. Chapter Three describes our work as a meandering journey, which will hopefully serve as an invitation.

Not many people leap onto our couches or into our chairs, or even understand our method of work, so degrees of explanation are in order, always tailored to the unique patient. Explanations have not been part of classical work, and I wonder why. Most analysts prefer interpretation, which tilts the field, putting the analyst on a higher plane. After a certain amount of time in therapy, it is the patient who will come up with ideas that contribute to growth.

People have a right to know something about what they're getting into, and the explanations offered and the ways they are offered can determine the outcome of a first meeting and even of a whole analysis. Everyone has stories to tell and the very act of telling them to an attentive listener promotes growth and solves mysteries. Sherlock Holmes also said: "Nothing clears up a case so much as stating it to another person" (Doyle, 1893). This holds true in working psychoanalytically where colleagues often see our blind spots. Enjoy Chapter Eleven on storytelling.

The fact that a person makes an appointment and keeps it indicates strength and courage. If we remember that each dyad is unique, improvisation is natural, and intuition guides us. Genuine spontaneity is important. Messiness is allowed when working this way, but the dyad works towards repair. Claudia Gold and Ed Tronick (2020) explore this idea in their book: *The Power of Discord.* This essential aspect of the dyad's work relies on the present, what we refer to as the *here and now* interaction, and it may even take precedence over revisiting the past. It may also include the past as reference point. *"This reminds me of the time when my sister was born and I was supposed to be the big girl all of a sudden,"* said one patient when discussing her experience at a new job. Her memory opened a new door quite naturally, a door that illustrated the past's influence on the present. *"You just sounded like my father"* said another patient leading to memories of a man who died long ago and who had not been mourned.

Psychoanalytic work is filled with stories, and I have found that at times the therapist's stories are a useful part of the relationship. We call this *self-disclosure,* and it has been frowned upon by classical analysts. Some might even call it a boundary crossing. But, when the analyst has something to share that is appropriate to what's going on, it seems only natural to do so, spontaneously and genuinely. I give an example in the Listening chapter. I think of my meeting with patients as containing both playfulness and heart-to-heart conversations along with my reflective capacity.

The therapist acts as a guide/companion on the trip of exploration. A crucial aspect of this journey is the motivation to inhabit the present, to envision the wished for or dreaded future while visiting the past when it sheds light on both. Exploring all three dimensions helps us understand ourselves without the need to master 'string theory' or 'time travel.' I think that saying *"That reminds me of xyz"* encourages us to use what comes to mind—what we call free association. Instead of making free association a rule, I see everything a patient says as free. And if he decides to withhold something, I assume he will figure out why as we go along. I have said to patients: *"As we meet, there will be things you wish to keep to yourself. When that happens, try thinking about why. What would happen if you just said whatever pops into your head?"* Usually, things withheld involve shame or lack of trust and as the bond strengthens, the patient will feel more comfortable sharing what she thinks. Motivation is enhanced by the rapport established—and it is up to the guide to set a tone of benevolent curiosity. Before trusting one's travel companion, a period of assessment and testing occurs, and each party uses both their conscious intelligence and their gut feelings to determine whether the trip feels safe enough to embark on together. I talk about this testing in the Chapter Three: Self-Murder.

Developing trust takes varying amounts of time but it is indispensable when traveling. Patients test us, consciously and unconsciously, so the frame is necessary because it guarantees safety.

I think of the dyad's work as a long conversation, or as solving mysteries together. These analogies help me explain what I do. Struggling to get an idea across can get messy. Ed Tronick points out that Fred Astaire and his partners surely stepped on each other's toes while practicing before their performances. We make mistakes and we recover. In the recovery lies the growth. And when we goof, we apologize.

I begin this book with my first experience as a therapist, still in social work school, with Chapter One: Let's Fall In Love. I wrote these chapters with love—for the field, the patients, my colleagues, and those who I supervise and teach. Love does make the world go round; we just have to find it. I would like to see us all more comfortable with the basic love we feel—the libido Martin Bergmann and I spoke about in Chapter Twelve.

I realize that many ideas show up in multiple chapters which is why skipping around or reading at your leisure is okay.

References

Barron, J.W., Beaumont, R., Goldsmith, G.N., Good, M.I., Pyles, R L., Rizzuto, A. & Smith, H. F. (1991). Sigmund Freud: The Secrets of Nature and the Nature of Secrets. *International Review of Psychoanalysis* 18:143–163.

Breger, L. (2009). *A Dream of Undying Fame: How Freud Betrayed His Mentor and Invented Psychoanalysis,* New York, Basic Books.

Bromberg, P.M. (1996). Standing in the Spaces: The Multiplicity of Self and The Psychoanalytic Relationship. *Contemporary Psychoanalysis* 32: 509–535.

Bowlby, J. (1980). *Attachment and Loss.* London: The International Psycho-Analytical Library.

Doidge, N. (2007). *The Brain That Changes Itself.* New York: Viking Books.

Doyle, A.C. (1894). *The Memoirs of Sherlock Holmes.* New York: Harper and Brothers.

Freud, S. (1926). The Question of Lay Analysis. *S.E.* 20:177–258.

Gay, P. (1988). *Freud: A Life For Our Time*. New York: W.W. Norton & Co.

Holtzman, D. & Kulish, N. (2000). The Femininization of the Female Oedipal Complex, Part I: A Reconsideration of the Significance of Separation Issues. *Journal of the American Psychoanalytic Association* 48:1413–1437.

Knight, R. (2021). Reconsidering Development in Psychoanalysis, *The Psychoanalytic Study of the Child*, 75:215–232.

Levine, R. (2016). *Stranger in the Mirror*. Boston: Little, Brown Spark.

Lee, P. (1946). *I Don't Know Enough About You. Santa Monica, CA: Universal Music-MGB Songs.* https://www.lyrics.com/lyric/1036832/Peggy+Lee/ I+Don%27t+Know+Enough+About+You.

McWilliams, N. (2011). *Psychoanalytic Diagnosis*. Guilford.

Nass, M. (1975). Personal Communication.

Ogden, T.H. (2007). Elements of analytic style: Bion's clinical seminars. *Int. J. Psychoanal.* 88: 1185–1200.

Pankseep, J., Biven, L., (2012). *The Archaeology of Mind. Neuroevolutionary Origins of Human Emotions*. New York & London: W.W. Norton & Company

Purcell, S. (2019). Psychic Song and Dance: Dissociation and Duets in the Analysis of Trauma. *The Psychoanalytic Quarterly* 88:2, 315–347.

Sharpe, E. (1950). *Collected Papers on Psychoanalysis*. London: Hogarth Press and The Institute of Psychoanalysis.

Simon, B. (1991). Is the Oedipus Complex Still the Cornerstone of Psychoanalysis? Three Obstacles to Answering the Question. *Journal of the American Psychoanalytic Association* 39:641–668

Solnit, R. (2014). Woolf's Darkness: Embracing The Inexplicable. *The New Yorker*, April 24.

Stone, L. (1954). The Widening Scope of Indications for Psychoanalysis. *Journal of the American Psychoanalytic Association* 2:567–594.

Tronick, E.Z., (2001). Emotional connections and dyadic consciousness in infant mother and patient-therapist interactions. *Psychoanalytic Dialogues* 11:187–194.

_____ & Beeghly, M. (2011). Infants' Meaning-making and the Development of Mental Health Problems. *American Psychologist* 66(2):107–119.

_____ & Process of Change Study Group, (1998). Dyadically expanded state of Consciousness and the Process of Therapeutic Change. *Infant Mental Health Journal* 19(3), 290–299.

Feeling Connected
On "Introduction and Philosophy"

Jon G. Allen

Jane Hall (2022) introduced *The Power of Connection* as a book of essays and riffs. As a jazz pianist, I use this commentary as an opportunity to riff on my current consternation with the field of psychotherapy. To my dismay, I write at an ironically apposite time: the immediate aftermath of the 2024 presidential election in the United States. Entering the ninth decade of my life, I have never witnessed a period of more pervasive divisiveness in this country. We must place our hope in the power of connection. We have much to learn from the field of psychotherapy, also a potential domain of connection while historically riven with polarization that continues to escalate (Allen, 2023).

Mainstream psychotherapy in the U.S. is dominated by countless variations of cognitive-behavior therapies, which have largely cornered the market of short-term, evidence-based, and manualized therapies. These therapies have been designed to treat codified psychiatric symptoms and disorders to qualify for reimbursement in the healthcare system. Patients who want time to talk with therapists about their personal problems—largely in a developmental context of problematic relationships—will generally pay out of pocket, greatly limiting access to what many of us construe as psychotherapy as it has long been practiced (McWilliams, 2023). The field has now been inundated with hundreds of therapies and decades of research consisting of horserace-like competitions that generally show little differences among therapies in effectiveness; meanwhile, decades of research has shown that the quality of the therapeutic relationship strongly influences treatment outcomes (Wampold & Imel, 2015). Moreover, individual differences among therapists contribute substantially to outcomes, especially in the treatment of more severely impaired patients (Castonguay & Hill, 2017). Accordingly, I have argued that we should shift our focus from developing more *therapies* to enhancing the development of *therapists* (Allen, 2022). Psychoanalysis excels here.

In recent years, the beginning therapists I have taught and supervised have been overwhelmed by their sense that they must scramble to learn myriad methods and techniques to treat a host of psychiatric conditions. They must document the "evidence-based" interventions they employed in the session. I aspire to completely reorient their thinking, with therapeutic relationships foremost in mind. I acknowledge their insistence that they must "play the game" in their documentation. But I tell them that they began developing the skills that will play the most important role in their effectiveness in infancy and that, by the time in early adulthood that they begin conducting psychotherapy, much of their crucial development has taken place. They will superimpose essential professional knowledge and skills on this development, and their personal development of relational skill will continue throughout their lifetime. Moreover, to be effective, their professional knowledge must be assimilated into their personal knowledge such that the methods they employ will feel natural and intuitive as they forge therapeutic relationships with their patients. Furthermore, they and their patients must come to *feel connected,* building on relational skills originating in infant-caregiver interactions.

Thanks also to decades of research, we are fully aware of infants' preverbal relational skills, albeit contingent on and intermingled with caregivers' skills. Incipiently feeling connected, infants engage in emotion sharing (Tomasello, 2019), and they learn strategies for optimizing their attachment needs (i.e., managing distress) depending on the individual caregiver's emotional responsiveness to these needs (Ainsworth, Blehar, Waters, & Wall, 1978). Thanks to Ed Tronick's (2007) groundbreaking research, we have learned that a predominance of disconnection is normative in infant-caregiver interactions (i.e., a 70:30 proportion); this disconnection is relatively transient, however, and is essential for both infant and caregiver to learn mutually adaptive strategies for restoring connection. From attachment research (Main & Morgan, 1996) we also have learned how pervasive disconnection can profoundly derail the capacity for connection and form the basis of developmental psychopathology that we treat more or less belatedly—albeit ideally in infancy and early childhood (Slade, Sadler, Eaves, & Webb, 2023). Although language is profoundly transformative in the development of social learning and emotional connections, these basic preverbal relational skills also continue to be refined over the later course of development and remain crucial in emotion sharing and feeling connected. We should bear in mind the obvious fact that all this developmental research is as pertinent to therapists' relational skills as it is to their patients. And all of us must appreciate that nothing is carved in stone to the extent that life can afford continuing opportunities for relational development, including our merely century-old cultural invention of psychotherapy (Sroufe, 2021). Accordingly, psychotherapy can be as crucial for therapists' development as it is for their patients (Orlinsky, 2022).

To my knowledge, the richest theoretical and clinical literature bearing on therapeutic relationships has evolved under the rubric of relational psychoanalysis (Mitchell & Aron,

1999; Seligman, 2018), which has long historical roots in psychoanalysis more broadly. Yet the influence of psychoanalysis on the field of psychotherapy has been constrained by enduring stereotypes of classical psychoanalyses as characterized by a relatively opaque analyst interpreting unconscious conflicts. The bane of this stereotype is the image of the therapist as emotionally detached—*feeling disconnected.* This recent relational literature has been transformative in offering concepts that illuminate the ever-developing feelings of connection that form the linchpin of therapeutic action. In what follows, I merely highlight the set of concepts that I find most helpful—and, in principle, applicable to all but the most rigidly manualized practices of psychotherapy. All these concepts entail a paradoxical synergy of togetherness and separateness, shared experience that preserves and enhances individual subjectivity. As Louis Sander (2008) articulated, "one of the central paradoxes in the developmental process," contrasts "the singularity, the uniqueness of each individual, each newborn, each family system, and each developmental pathway" with "intersubjectivity; that is, how we are each a part of the other." His central question: "How can we both be a part of each other and singularly unique at the same time?" (p. 178). And, from my phenomenological point of view, the feeling of connection is *ineffable,* although we can point our attention to it with language (Merleau-Ponty, 2012; Vygotsky, 1934/2012). Four concepts seem particularly helpful to me: recognition, the analytic Third, the interpersonal field, and implicit relational knowing. In each case, the authors cited provide extensive clinical examples that point to the relevant experience.

Recognition. We ordinarily use the word, recognition, to refer to a unidirectional process; one person identifies another as familiar, or a group accords admiration to an individual for an achievement. In the relational psychoanalytic literature, by contrast, recognition is an interpersonal, reciprocal process. It is intersubjective, as Sander (2008) articulated, emphasizing the *specificity* of the experience of recognition in unique moments of connection, that is, the "specificity in *another's awareness of what we experience being aware of within ourselves.*" (p. 184, emphasis added). Jessica Benjamin (2018) masterfully integrated the experience of connection with the sense of separateness:

> Acts of recognition confirm that I am seen, known, my intentions have been understood, I have had an impact on you, and this must also mean that *I matter to you;* and reciprocally, that I see and know you, I understand your intentions, your actions affect me, and *you matter to me.* Further, we share feelings, reflect each other's knowing, so we also have shared awareness. This is recognition. (p. 4, emphasis added)

We have connection and togetherness that preserves and enhances individuality. I am especially interested in the *connector* and the feeling of connection, as described in complementary ways: most straightforwardly, the "We" between the "I" and "You." I start there and then proceed to the more abstract concepts of the interpersonal field and the Third.

We. Envision a triangle with I and You at the base connecting to We at the apex. Michael Tomasello (2019) traces the development of a "sense of We" (p. 196) over the course of toddlerhood and early childhood (one-to-two and three-to-six years of age, respectively). In a similar vein, Peter Fonagy and colleagues (Fonagy et al., 2021) refer to the "feeling of 'We-ness'" (p. 6) and interacting in the "we-mode" as "the shared thinking and feeling within a social system, a dyad, a family, or other social group" (p. 6). Fonagy (2022) asserts that "there is no mysterious leap into a mystical interpersonal space of 'we-ness;'" rather, "the we mode is *an individual state* characterized by voluntary subsuming of the I mode into one where the dominant goal is joint action and collaboration" (p. xiv, emphasis added). I am in the we-mode and you are in the we-mode. No connector.

Interpersonal Field. Donnel Stern (D. B. Stern, 1983) views the interpersonal connection as an enveloping field of influence, jointly created by the analyst and patient and either enabling or constraining what each can experience in their being together. The interpersonal field is the "sum total of all influences, conscious and unconscious, that each of the analytic participants exerts on the other" as well as "the outcome of all those influences, relatedness and experience created between the two" (pp. 187-188). Stern appreciates the ineffable quality of the field; it is "emergent," "unbidden," and imbued with "mystery" (p. 252). Ideally and therapeutically, the field promotes spontaneity, creativity, and openness to previously unexpressed or defensively prohibited experience. Such a field creates a paradoxical *negative capability:* "being in uncertainties, mysteries, doubts, without any irritable reaching after fact and reason" (p. 255). Recognition entails *inter*-subjectivity, and the field is *inter*-personal. At the risk of reification (concretizing an abstraction), I puzzle: What is in the space between the individuals?

The Third. Substitute "the Third" for "We" of the apex of the I-You-We triangle. We have two individuals (separateness) and a connector, the Third (togetherness). Thomas Ogden (1999) envisioned a "third subjectivity, the intersubjective third," that "coexists in dynamic tension with the analyst and the analysand as separate individuals with their own thoughts, feelings, sensations, corporal reality, psychological identity and so on" (p. 463). Further, "The analytic third is a *creation* of the analyst and the analysand, and at the same time, the analyst and analysand…are *created by* the analytic third" (p. 483, emphasis added). Here Ogden makes a crucial point: In the meeting of minds occurrent in the Third, *the creation creates the creators.*

Implicit Relational Knowing. Infant research provides solid scientific backing for my contention that we begin developing the interpersonal skills essential to conducting psychotherapy early in life (Amadei & Bianchi, 2008; D. N. Stern, 1985). I would hope that none of us talk therapists harbor any illusions about the limited impact of insight on behavior change. But I imagine that few of us focus merely on behavior change (or cognitive change, for that matter). Along with our patients, many of us aspire to understanding and being understood; such understanding is valuable in itself and, as recognition and related concepts attest, mutuality in understanding contributes to feeling connected. With the basis of therapeutic change in mind, Daniel Stern and his colleagues (Boston Change Process Study Group, 2010) brought the experience of connection to the foreground in prioritizing shifts in implicit relational knowing, put simply: "the sense, based on one's history, of *how to be* with another" (p. 145, emphasis added). This preverbal and nonverbal way of knowing continues to develop in parallel to explicit (verbal-reflective) knowledge over the lifetime: "the implicit domain continues to grow in breadth and elaboration with age. Implicit knowledge is a *far larger domain* of knowing about human behavior than explicit knowledge at all ages, not just in infancy" (p. 147, emphasis added). Getting to the heart of feeling connected as pivotal in psychotherapy, Stern (D. N. Stern, 2004) focuses on present moments: *"The moment of meeting* need not be verbalized to effectuate change. A now moment followed by a moment of meeting is the nodal event that can dramatically change a relationship or the course of a therapy" (p. 220).

In prioritizing the *feeling* of connection, I do not aim to diminish the role of language in human relational life but rather wish to elevate the value of experience. In his critique of empiricism in science, Gabriel Marcel (2018) expressed my sentiment beautifully: we "take experience for granted and ignore its mystery; whereas *what is amazing and miraculous is that there should be experience at all"* (p. 140, emphasis added). Preoccupied with thinking, problem solving, and planning, we lose sight of experience. Marcel argued instead that experience should be "not so much a springboard as a *promised land"* (p. 115). At best, we are able to translate only a tiny fraction of our experience into words (Merleau-Ponty, 2012), and any efforts to do so will fall short to varying degrees (Vygotsky, 1934/2012). Moreover, as psychoanalysis attests, efforts to translate experience into words often will run into defenses. As Donnel Stern (D. B. Stern, 1983) elucidates compellingly, a cornerstone of psychoanalytic practice entails *formulating unformulated experience*, and doing so will require establishing a conducive interpersonal field. Ideally, such formulation (e.g., verbal reflection) will expand and enhance the range of experience rather than detracting from it (e.g., as intellectualization will do).

In closing, I address the impetus for this commentary, explicating controversies that have been implicit, including prioritizing treating psychiatric disorders versus the experience of life and the role of interpretation and insight versus the experience of relating. Here I lodge a protest against scientism, characterized by Barbara Herrnstein Smith (2009) as the conviction that "the natural sciences should be taken as models for all knowledge practices," coupled with the presumption that "the humanities disciplines are at best pre-scientific and should be shepherded as quickly as possible, along with some still vagrant social sciences, into the fold of the natural sciences" (p. 20). As applied to psychotherapy, scientism is anathema in its aspiration to "cancel out the personal, subjective, social and political; to arrive at an accurate, undistorted representation of nature" (Smith, 2006, p. 58), while employing "depersonalized ideas stated in special technical terms, *'a language estranged from life'* " (p. 68, emphasis added). My contrary stance: Science's majesty does not entitle it to a monarchy (Allen, 2023).

I believe that a scientistic ideology hampers our appreciation of the feeling of connection. To reiterate, I am intrigued by the *connector* that constitutes recognition, the interpersonal field, and the Third. Consider that many of us therapists are in the *psych* fields: psychiatry, psychology, psychotherapy, and psychoanalysis. The *psyche* refers to soul and spirit. Setting religion aside, we can refer to the *mind*. Enamored with more scientific terminology, we turned from mind to *cognition*. Embracing science and avoiding reification, we can construe connection (the "We") as lodged in individual minds. But we can go full bore into scientism by concentrating on the *brain*. We have ample philosophical precedent for this counterintuitive perspective by construing human experience as an illusion, in effect, a theater created by the brain (Humphrey, 2011). We now have on offer Right Brain Psychotherapy, a way *"to understand the relational mechanisms by which communicating brains align and synchronize their neural activities with other brains"* (Schore, 2019, emphasis in original). Who or what is connecting with whom or what? Ignoring the brain's embeddedness in the body and the world leaves us imprisoned in our skulls—disconnected and alienated from human life (Fuchs, 2018, 2021). In our scientistic zeitgeist, allusion to the brain has become *de rigeur*. I find neuroscience to be fascinating and unquestionably valuable in its own right. But what I know about the brain has not helped me understand the person in front of me. Perhaps I don't know enough. Do You?

I criticize reductionistic thinking as I bristle at the constraints of scientism. My interest in feeling connected has brought this contrarian way of thinking to the fore. As a jazz pianist, I welcome the limits of verbal reflection along with the power of art as a medium of expression and understanding (Dewey, 1934; Taylor, 2016). I revel in the sense of mystery and propose the best word to capture my experience of connection: *spiritual*. Back to the psyche.

References

Ainsworth, M. D. S., Blehar, M. C., Waters, E., & Wall, S. (1978). *Patterns of attachment: A psychological study of the strange situation*. Hillsdale, NJ: Erlbaum.

Allen, J. G. (2022). *Trusting in psychotherapy*. Washington, DC: American Psychiatric Publishing.

Allen, J. G. (2023). Contending with polarization in the expanding scope of psychotherapy. *Journal of Psychiatric Practice, 29*, 378–383.

Allen, J.G. (2025) *Bringing Psychotherapy to Life through Caring Connections,* American Psychiatric Publishing (in press).

Amadei, G., & Bianchi, I. (Eds.). (2008). *Living systems, evolving consciousness, and the emerging person: A selection of papers from the life work of Louis Sander.* New York: Routledge.

Benjamin, J. (2018). *Beyond doer and done to: Recognition theory, intersubjectivity and the third.* New York: Routledge.

Boston Change Process Study Group. (2010). *Change in psychotherapy: A unifying paradigm.* New York: Norton.

Castonguay, L. G., & Hill, C. E. (Eds.). (2017). *How and why are some therapists better than others?* Washington, DC: American Psychological Association.

Dewey, J. (1934). *Art as Experience.* New York: Penguin.

Fonagy, P. (2022). Foreword. In J. G. Allen (Ed.), *Trusting in Psychotherapy* (pp. xi–xviii). Washington, D.C.: American Psychiatric Publishing.

Fonagy, P., Campbell, C., Constantinou, M., Higgitt, A., Allison, E., & Luyten, P. (2021). Culture and psychopathology: An attempt at reconsidering the role of social learning. *Development and Psychopathology, 34,* 1–16.

Fuchs, T. (2018). *Ecology of the Brain.* New York: Oxford University Press.

Fuchs, T. (2021). *In Defense of the Human Being: Foundational Questions of an Embodied Anthropology.* New York: Oxford University Press.

Hall, J. (2022). *The Power of Connection.* Unknown: International Psychoanalytic Books.

Humphrey, Nicholas. (2011). *Soul Dust: The magic of consciousness.* Princeton, NJ: Princeton University Press.

Main, M., & Morgan, H. (1996). Disorganization and disorientation in infant Strange Situation behavior: Phenotypic resemblance to dissociative states. In L. K. Michelson & W. J. Ray (Eds.), *Handbook of dissociation: Theoretical, empirical, and clinical perspectives* (pp. 107–138). New York: Plenum.

Marcel, G. (2018). *The philosophy of existence*. Providence, RI: Cluny Media.

McWilliams, N. (2023). Diagnosis and its discontents: Reflections on our current dilemma. In L. Michaels, T. Wooldridge, N. Burke, & J. R. Muhr (Eds.), *Advancing Psychotherapy for the Next Generation: Humanizing mental health policy and practice* (pp. 162–181). New York: Routledge.

Merleau-Ponty, M. (2012). *The Phenomenology of Perception* (D. A. Landes, Trans.). New York: Routledge.

Mitchell, S. A., & Aron, L. (Eds.). (1999). *Relational psychoanalysis: The emergence of a tradition*. New York: Routledge.

Orlinsky, D.E. (2022). *How Psychotherapists Live: The personal self and private life of professional healers*. New York: Routledge.

Sander, L. (2008). Recognition processes: Context and experience of being known. In G. Amadei & I. Bianchi (Eds.), *Living Systems, Evolving Consciousness, and the Emerging Person: A selection of papers from the life and work of Louis Sander* (pp. 177–192). New York: Routledge.

Schore, A. N. (2019). *Right Brain Psychotherapy*. New York: Norton.

Seligman, S. (2018). *Relationships in development: Infancy, intersubjectivity, and attachment*. New York: Routledge.

Slade, A., Sadler, L. S., Eaves, T., & Webb, D. L. (2023). *Enhancing attachment and reflective parenting: A Minding The Baby approach*. New York: Guilford.

Smith, B. H. (2006). *Scandalous Knowledge: Science, Truth and the Human*. Durham, NC: Duke University Press.

Smith, B. H. (2009). *Natural Reflections: Human Cognition at the Nexus of Science and Religion*. New Haven, CT: Yale University Press.

Sroufe, A. (2021). *A Compelling Idea: How We Become the Persons We Are*. Brandon, VT: Safer Society Press.

Stern, D. B. (1983). Unformulated experience: From familiar chaos to creative disorder. *Contemporary Psychoanalysis, 19,* 71–99.

Stern, D. N. (1985). *The interpersonal world of the infant: A view from psychoanalysis and developmental psychology*. New York: Basic Books.

Stern, D. N. (2004). *The present moment in psychotherapy and everyday life*. New York: Norton.

Taylor, C. (2016). *The Language Animal: The full shape of the human linguistic capacity*. Cambridge, MA: Harvard University Press.

Tomasello, M. (2019). *Becoming human: A theory of ontogeny*. Cambridge, MA: Harvard University Press.

Tronick, E. (2007). *The neurobehavioral and social-emotional development of infants and children*. New York: Norton.

Vygotsky, L. (1934/2012). *Thought and Language* (E. Hanfmann, G. Vakar, & A. Kozulin, Trans.). Cambridge, MA: MIT Press.

Wampold, B. E., & Imel, Z. E. (2015). *The great psychotherapy debate: The evidence for what makes psychotherapy work* (Second ed.). New York: Routledge.

A Brief Note on "Let's Fall In Love"

M. Sagman Kayatekin

"I know no other word to describe what I feel. Love is made up of respect, enthusiasm, passion, platonic and erotic feelings, curiosity, caring, compassion, and deep appreciation that offsets the disillusionment that can lie in wait."

A shy and moral 'junkie'

Hall starts this collection with an inspiring story from the times when she was a young and inexperienced social worker in Psychoanalytic training.

"Greenwich House Counseling Center in the early 1970s.... I will always remember him—a middle aged, African American, homeless man, required to come to my clinic by the welfare department.... Mr. S. seemed to have lost everything."

It was an accidental meeting of two persons, a young therapist and a patient. They both were assigned to the counseling center and to one another. Probably because of the involuntary nature of the beginning, there was some added oddness and anxiety in the air. Yet the therapist-patient pair seem to have developed an immediate interest in one another. Albeit an awkward one.

Hall was gently persistent in her pursuit to establish a human tie; she isn't pushed away easily despite the overt disinterest and some assaulting remarks of the patient. Patient says how would a *"white chick—have nice clothes, a job, probably a family—how can my talking to you have any meaning?"* When Hall gently perseveres, with some hesitation, S. reveals a secret. He is worried that Hall would despise him because he was stealing money to buy drugs and spent time in jail because of that. Hall in turn makes a comment that feels like a turning point. She says her job is not to judge him and asks whether the two of them could be curious as to how to make sense of what happened to him. After many such mini battles patient probably notices, what Hall calls 'love' of his new therapist. S. leaves with her card as he mumbles a thank you on his way out.

As we all know, the 'doorknob comments' that our patients make on their way out are quite important. They usually provide a synoptic summary, in a few words, of what they didn't or couldn't articulate in the whole 50 minutes prior to leaving. Like a deeply shy person perhaps.

There are stories of very shy persons, some of them quite famous, who have declared their love to another person by scribbling the loving words on a piece of paper and showing it to the person. In times when it was not frowned upon, a cigarette package was one common and easily accessible surface to write a short love note on. One has a fleeting impression that the doorknob mumble of S. was one such scribbling.

I and we

A second section is a short story about adventures in the land of groups. Jane has a deep trust in human capacity to heal and thus she is not too embarrassed over her being a novice, an authentic and open one, and utilizes her professional naivete with her probably very old apprenticeship in helping others. Thus, a fascinating short section comes out early on, in the book.

"I had no training in group work, so I was flying blind. I began by introducing myself to seven men between age fifty and sixty-five.

We sat in a circle and after each of us said our names, I told some of my story first—that I was studying to be a psychoanalyst. 'What's that?' one man asked. They were curious so I told them about what I was learning—specifically how one's past can affect the present and how memories are often stored in the unconscious part of the mind. ...Telling and listening to each other's stories was something they had never experienced. These men had been essentially alone."

Hall continues; *"Well, the first thing about analytic work is getting interested in the "whys" or "reasons" for what we do in life with benevolent curiosity. It opens a new door. But even more important, connecting to a trusted other can be lifesaving"..."Gentlemen, I have one request and that is to replace all criticism with curiosity."*

Perhaps for the first time these men paid and received attention in positive ways. We tend to forget that attention without judgement is what we all want—from birth and throughout life.

Hall wonderfully demonstrates how these patients found the stories of each other absorbing, and that lead to an interest and courage to tell their own.

We do become individuals as we feel like a part of a group. This "I in the we" opens the key to adolescence identities or any group for that matter. It raises the perennial question of how one may lose their individuality in a group that leads to what they mistakenly call group regressions, and mass hatred/violence. At the same time, one may find a core sense of individuality, selfhood in a group. So what is the difference is the natural question that follows.

A major difference probably is, the former is a group of differentiated, unique individuals focused on each other as friends. Latter is group of undifferentiated members focused on other groups as the enemy.

Loving anger

We are in a profession that carries a powerful tone of helpfulness and benevolence. Which is quite prone to create an almost prototypical image of an all loving, endlessly tolerant therapist. Jane counters it.

> *"I remember raising my voice in exasperation at my first analytic patient who had been complaining and raging at me for weeks. I was in supervision at the time and dreaded telling my supervisor that one day I angrily said: "Stop! I have listened to these complaints and insults for long enough. Now is the time to figure out what they mean—to figure out who, why, and what you're really talking about." The supervisor, to my surprise, said it was about time!"*

We tend to easily forget that Freud used plenty references to battle and war. Which is a striking contrast to the benevolent peaceful image of the therapist. Jane reminds us that, those may coexist, a spirit of a fighter and a spirit of a helper.

Winnicott talks about the ordinary hatred of the mother. Despite our wishes to underplay it, what he refers to is a real genuine hatred.

Or as Otto Will remembers in his analysis with Sullivan:

"And I said to him in anger, 'I'm so angry I could throw you out the window.' " And he said, 'No doubt you could.' And later, when I got up to leave, I felt embarrassed and kind of ashamed of myself and I said, 'You're really not like my father. My father used to say 'no' to me in a certain way that seems an awful lot like you do, so I suppose my anger is an example of father transference.' Sullivan said, 'No Doctor, I don't think so. I think at the moment you don't like me very much, and at the moment I don't care very much for you either!' (Thompson and Thomson 1998)

'Hall' ian love

With the section "Lets fall in love" we begin reading the story of Jane Hall, a young person who is interested in and curious about other human beings. 'S.', 'members of the group', 'the patient Hall yells at.'

All of these were relationships embedded in love, and they have lived forever in Halls mind, as evidenced by their freshness after so many decades. She later on improvises on the central tune/theme of 'love' and uses different names—caritas, benevolent curiosity and such. All of which seem to be connected, similar and yet different. Just like the improvisations of her late beloved husband, the prominent jazz guitarist and musician Jim Hall.

Jane Hall uses love in a unique way. Unique in the sense that it is re-discovered, time and again, by every new generation of analyst/therapists. It is an all-encompassing love that floods well beyond the walls of our colloquial usages. *"The way I see it, non-transferential love in the consulting room, not often talked about, happens over time. It does not preclude frustration or anger."*

One is reminded of Winnicott. "Regarding 'analytic love', it may be asked whether Loewald uses the term as the opposite of hate in the conventional sense, or whether, like Winnicott, he uses it to speak of a quality of acceptance and attunement that contains and facilitates, a quality that more or less *transcends* love or hate in the ordinary sense." (Fogel, 1996 pp 898).

Hall suggests that this is a capacity that can be considered as innate. As is well depicted in some forgotten notion of

Sigmund Freud, the 'effective transference.' "It remains the first aim of the treatment to attach him to it and to the person of the doctor. To ensure this, nothing need be done but to give him time. If one exhibits a serious interest in him, carefully clears away the resistances that crop up at the beginning and avoids making certain mistakes, he will of himself form such an attachment and link the doctor up with one of the imagos of the people by whom he was accustomed." (Freud S., 1913, pp 139).

In this chapter and the rest of the book, we will follow the meanderings of what happens. I would say, Hall describes, in her unique and evocative way what happens when the shadow of the object falls on the ego. (Freud S., 1917).

References

Fogel, G. I., Tyson, P., Greenberg, J., McLaughlin, J. T. & Peyser, E. R. (1996). A Classic Revisited: Loewald on The Therapeutic Action of Psychoanalysis. *Journal of the American Psychoanalytic Association* 44:863–924. 898

Freud, S. (1913). On Beginning the Treatment (Further Recommendations on the Technique of Psycho-Analysis I). *The Standard Edition of the Complete Psychological Works of Sigmund Freud* 12:121–144. 139

_____ (1917). Mourning and Melancholia. *The Standard Edition of the Complete Psychological Works of Sigmund Freud* 14:237–258. 249

Thompson, M. G. & Thompson, S. (1998) Interview with Dr. Otto Allen Will, Jr. *Contemporary Psychoanalysis* 34:289–304. 292

A New Way of Thinking About Developmental Theory and Treatment in Psychoanalysis

Rona Knight

Jane Hall's conceptualization of therapeutic work and the mechanisms of change aligns closely with my own understanding of psychoanalytic treatment. It also underscores the necessity of continually evaluating our theories of development, practice, and technique—distinguishing what remains valuable from what requires modification. My theoretical framework has evolved into developmental psychoanalysis, informed significantly by nonlinear dynamic systems theory. This perspective emerged from a longitudinal research project I initiated in the 1980s (Knight, 2005, 2011).

Rethinking Latency: A Longitudinal Study

I undertook a longitudinal study to gain a deeper understanding of the developmental phase historically referred to as latency. Traditional descriptions characterized this period as one of relative calm and malleability—an image that starkly contrasted with the children I encountered in clinical settings. To investigate this discrepancy, I followed nine neurotypical boys and girls from age five to twelve, collecting annual psychological test data, structured interviews, parent and teacher questionnaires, and videotaped peer interactions.

Initially, my study design was based on psychosexual theory. However, upon analysis, the data did not conform to the conventional psychosexual model of latency. While some expected findings emerged, the children's psychological development displayed complexities that defied traditional conceptualizations. The data remained unexamined for years until I discovered nonlinear dynamic systems theory, which Thelen and Smith (1994) had employed in motor development research. This framework provided a way to reinterpret my findings and demonstrated how dynamic systems theory can enrich psychoanalytic understandings of development.

Nonlinear Development:
Disruptions and Transformations

To illustrate the complexity of nonlinear dynamic systems, I will report several key developmental patterns identified in my research. Boys at age six and girls at age seven exhibited ego fragmentation, triggered by the confluence of separation-individuation processes, cognitive shifts, and hormonal fluctuations. Core internal structures, such as gender identity, became fluid, and both sexual and aggressive impulses intensified. By age eight, defenses described by Sigmund and Anna Freud (1936) reached sufficient maturity to manage these impulses. However, by age nine, these defenses unpredictably broke down, leading to a transient period of internal chaos. Projective testing revealed that children at this age displayed psychotic-like cognition, with conscious concerns about hallucinations and delusions.

At age ten, equilibrium was briefly restored before a subsequent fragmentation period emerged—particularly among girls entering pre-puberty. Notably, boys, who had not yet reached this hormonal stage, did not exhibit the same level of fragmentation, reinforcing the notion of distinct biological clocks for male and female development. By age eleven, both boys and girls navigating another phase of separation-individuation displayed depressive symptoms and suicidal ideation in projective testing, mourning the real and anticipated loss of childhood.

These findings suggest that development is neither linear nor predictable. Instead, it is characterized by cyclical disruptions and reorganizations—patterns observed across species, from primitive organisms to humans (Sander, 2002). Importantly, individuals rely on self-organizing and self-regulating structures, fostered within structured, supportive environments, to navigate these recurrent phases of disequilibrium.

Implications for Psychoanalytic Theory and Practice

For over three decades, research in neuropsychology, cognitive science, and socio-emotional development has demonstrated that psychological growth is shaped by dynamic interactions between biological, cognitive, and environmental factors. Thelen (1994) asserts, "Development can only be understood as the multiple, mutual, and continuous interaction of all levels of the developing system, from the molecular to the cultural." My research substantiates this claim, illustrating how development is fluid, nonlinear, and responsive to shifting internal and external conditions.

Periods of structural disorganization are not anomalies but essential components of growth. Stable cognitive, emotional, and biological configurations frequently destabilize, giving rise to transient fragmentation before new, more complex integrations emerge. Growth, therefore, is best understood through the increasing complexity and coherence of these reorganizing systems over time.

Another finding of my research is the occurrence of feelings of separation and individuation at many points in development not just in toddlerhood and adolescence. These feelings occur at every major developmental change: in toddlerhood, at the beginning of middle childhood, at the beginning of adolescence, at the beginning and end of emerging adulthood and throughout adulthood as people experience major bio-logical/social/psychological changes and losses in their lives. Encountering these feelings in adulthood is not a regression but a reaction to the environment and their developmental age.

A significant implication of this model is that regression does not occur. Rather than a return to earlier developmental stages, each phase of psychological and cognitive development is incorporated into higher-order transformations. Consequently, psychoanalytic treatment must prioritize present-moment interventions that enhance flexible defenses, adaptive relational patterns, and evolving self-narratives that support continued developmental progression.

Clinical Applications:
A New Paradigm for Psychoanalytic Treatment

This research supports a nonlinear dynamic systems approach to development, challenging longstanding notions of predictable, stage-based progression. It suggests that normal development is best understood as continuous disequilibrium, extending from infancy through adulthood—occurring during periods in which biological and psychological transformations remain in flux. Adolescence and emerging adulthood, in particular, exemplify nonlinear reorganization, as the brain and body undergo further dramatic changes.

A dynamic systems approach points out an important flaw in all the early theories about development, one that carries on today in other more contemporary theories of development. That is the idea of development being unduly influenced by the first two years of life—the overly influential relationship between the baby/toddler and her mother—leaving out the importance of the father, siblings, extended family, caretakers, teachers and peers, and the present and changing environment and culture on the continual psychological development of the infant, child, adolescent, emerging adult and adult.

One might ask how thoughts and mental representations are formed using a dynamic systems theory. Children initially perceive and internalize patterns of behavior from the people in their environment. As this social system develops, children make clear predictions about occurrences in their world and other people's actions based on their recognition of their own learned social behaviors and observations of the physical world. Representations held in memory reflect the structure of the environment and the temperament of the child because they are mapped to one's perceptions of the outside world. This allows internal representations to become meaningful in and of themselves through their use in interpreting the environment, making the child's thoughts and actions central to his understanding of the world he lives in. This is how conscious narratives are formed as the child, adolescent, emerging adult and adult continue to develop. It also makes clear the importance of working with the family to understand the mindset and interactions that the child and adolescent has observed and learned from.

Intelligence, internal representations, fantasies, morality and the unconscious can then be understood through *an integrative perspective* of the environment, the body and the mind and the degree to which these complex dynamic systems can stably engage and flexibly switch over a certain period of time. With the idea of systems continuously changing we can begin to study the ways in which the development of self and self-other representations, sexual and aggressive feelings, ego structures and moral development both change and *interweave* during every phase of development.

Stability and flexibility are both important if psychological growth is to occur. A system that is too variable would not be adaptable, because stability is necessary for change to have a chance to stabilize and reorganize. But a system that is *too* stable can result in constriction that does not allow for change and growth.

Each person brings her own innate strengths and vulnerabilities the physical, dispositional, neurobiological, and relational—to respond to and act upon the environmental system, all working together in a continuous reorganizational flow and transformation. Thus, it is the interaction of *multiple systems* that continually act in concert and change over time that evolve in the course of development. *All* phases of development are predominantly in a state of fluid linear and non-linear transformation that can be continuous and discontinuous. Through each stage of development there is a fragmentation period in which old structures break down and are changed by biology and the environment which includes their family and the culture of the time they are living in. Development is *messy*. It is filled with *novelty and complexity*, with both *parallel and interacting processes*. Major cognitive and biological changes are *continually* transforming a person's mind and body. Relational and environmental changes occur from infancy through old age. Culture is continually changing and influences development and a sense of self and other.

A dynamic systems theory allows analysts more freedom of thought. When I have presented this theory, I have heard more than one analyst say to me that they finally understood why they never felt comfortable with psychoanalytic theory—it felt too constricting in their work—and that a dynamic systems theory gave them permission to think more flexibly about all aspects of a patient's life.

Another advantage of *this* theory is that it supports the idea of people continually changing and growing *throughout* their life span. If we are flexible within ourselves and in our interactions with the world—both relationally, socially and culturally—our psychological/biological/cognitive systems are never "set" at a particular time in development. When I teach this to candidates, they are always relieved and hopeful because *this* theory recognizes that continual change is possible throughout development and makes the idea of change in analytic treatment achievable.

Conceptualizing development as a nonlinear dynamic system alters the way we think about the developmental organization of each person we work with and the treatment that will best help them. This requires us to give up the comfort of what we know and sit with the possibilities that arise with not knowing. Rather than focus on *genetic determinants* and think of present-day analytic interactions as *"regressive,"* I suggest that we attend to and analyze the *observable interaction in the analytic relationship* in the *present*, that can influence *further development* and *be influenced by* further development. Our job then becomes one of helping change our patient's story about him or herself by helping them reflect on what is *preventing* them from flexibly adapting to *present and future* developmental fluidity and reorganization. In this way, we can co-create a new narrative that promotes transformation and a more flexible and resilient development. Successful adaptation to biological, psychological, and environmental changes necessitates the capacity for flexible responses and the endurance of developmental disequilibrium. Novick and Novick (2003) conceptualize this adaptability through a two-system model: a closed system resists change, maintaining rigid defenses, while an open system accommodates new experiences, fostering ego resilience and developmental progression. From this perspective, persistent symptoms and character rigidity may indicate developmental pathology rather than stability.

Using dynamic systems theory and what we know about development helps our understanding and treatment of the children, adolescents, emerging adults and adults whom we treat. Sam Abrams (2003) suggested a non-hierarchical partnership in discovering, one in which the interpersonal "reflects an operational feature of the treatment relationship, [and] the intrapsychic defines how that operational feature is experienced in the minds of both participants." This definition is in keeping with Robert Galatzer-Levy's (1995) suggestion that operational descriptions devoid of semantic definitions like "mother" and "infant" are more likely to allow complex systems to arise from a dyadic exchange that is often filled with periods of disorganized, messy, not knowing that both participants have to tolerate.

Out of this interchange the analysand and the analyst are free to make new discoveries that are very particular to both people in the dyad. This is a model that rather than looking *backward* to genetic interpretation, looks *forward* to new developmental, emergent growth—something child analysts have *always* done but can also serve as a model for adult analysis. It requires keeping an eye on the present and the future rather than to experiences of the past or the nature of the equipment alone. While genetic interpretations might provide a narrative that gives a person a sense of continuity, they may not be accurate, and, more importantly, they short circuit a necessary understanding of the unconscious dynamics that are the product of interactional systems that help a person cope with their present life situation, for better or worse.

This way of looking at development complicates the task of understanding each patient in analysis since there is no prevailing central narrative, nor an expectable sequence that can be tracked. It requires each analysis to be a novel understanding, a novel narrative that is different for every person and analytic pair. The analytic relationship helps our patients make increasingly complex and coherent meanings of themselves, the analytic relationship and the environment in which they live. Each analysis becomes a process of discovery, a puzzle to be understood that is tailored to each individual we treat.

Treatment becomes a transforming and transformative partnership exploring the multiple determinants of psychological thinking and behavior, with the aim of bringing together an adaptive narrative that serves ongoing and future needs and values. This was Anna Freud's distinction between the developmental and genetic points of view.

Feeling understood by the analyst and understanding the analyst assists in the organization of the patient's feelings and thoughts. Feeling understood also provides a new level of relational and intrapsychic integration as the patient assimilates the understanding of new thoughts and feelings within the co-constructed narrative. The child or adult can then accommodate old systems of feeling and thinking to the new information, which leads to further development through structure building. Helping patients construct a narrative through play encourages the development of mentalization, facilitating the understanding and internal representation of self and other and furthers brain development.

Shifting to a nonlinear model requires relinquishing the assumption of orderly, stage-based progression. In return, we gain a framework that better accounts for the complexities of psychological development, paving the way for innovative clinical approaches. Embracing developmental ambiguity not only fosters new psychoanalytic research avenues but also refines our clinical understanding of "normal" progression.

From a treatment standpoint, conceptualizing development as a nonlinear process alters how we work with child, adolescent, and adult patients. Rather than focusing on genetic determinants or interpreting analytic interactions as regressive, I propose that we center our interventions on the observable present-day narrative. This includes examining how patients construct their self-understanding in relation to others and how these narratives shape ongoing development. Our task as analysts is to co-construct new narratives that expand the patient's adaptive capacities, helping them navigate future developmental reorganizations with greater fluidity.

Interdisciplinary Collaboration and Integration

NLDST goes beyond psychoanalysis, providing a framework that connects multiple disciplines. To keep psychoanalysis relevant in our rapidly changing world, we must engage with related fields. Neuroscience provides critical insights into the biological foundations of behavior, including the role of neuroplasticity in adaptation and growth. Developmental psychology contributes empirical research on attachment, learning, and resilience among others, while cultural studies enrich our understanding of the sociocultural contexts in which development occurs. Collaborating with researchers from these disciplines helps ensure that psychoanalytic theories stay scientifically valid and applicable.

By integrating these diverse perspectives, NLDST ensures that psychoanalytic theory remains scientifically grounded and clinically effective. This interdisciplinary approach not only enhances the validity of psychoanalytic models but also expands their applicability to diverse populations and contexts. As psychoanalysis embraces this modern framework it positions itself as a forward-looking field capable of addressing the complexities of human growth across the lifespan, ensuring that our field remains a vital and impactful discipline for understanding and supporting human potential.

Conclusion

By integrating nonlinear dynamic systems theory into psychoanalytic developmental theory, we gain a richer, more nuanced understanding of psychological growth. Recognizing development as an iterative process of organization, disorganization, and reorganization enables clinicians to more effectively address patients' adaptive and maladaptive responses to change. Rather than viewing psychological stability as the absence of disruption, we must reconceptualize it as the capacity to endure and integrate change—a shift that has profound implications for both psychoanalytic research and practice.

References

Abrams, S. (2003). Looking forwards and backwards. *Psychoanalytic Study of the Child, 58,* 172–186.

Freud, A. (1936). *The ego and the mechanisms of defense.* New York: International Universities Press.

Galatzer-Levy, R. (1995). Psychoanalysis and dynamic systems theory: Prediction and self-similarity. *Journal of the American Psychoanalytic Association, 43,* 1085–1113.

Knight, R.B. (2005). The process of attachment and autonomy in latency: A longitudinal study of ten children. *The Psychoanalytic Study of the Child, 60,* 178–210.

_____ (2011) Fragmentation, Fluidity, and transformation: Nonlinear development in middle childhood. *Psychoanalytic Study of the Child, 65,* 19–47.

Novick, K. K., & Novick, J. (2003). Two systems of self-regulation and the differential application of psychoanalytic technique. *American Journal of Psychoanalysis, 63*(1), 1–20.

Sander, L.W. (2002). Thinking differently: Principles of process in living systems and the specificity of being known. *Psychoanalytic Dialogues, 12*(1), 11–42.

Thelen, E., & Smith, L.B. (1994). *A dynamic systems approach to the development of cognition and action.* Cambridge, MA: MIT Press.

How We Do, and Talk About, Therapy
On "Self-murder"

David Cooper

In responding to this chapter, I want to start with an appreciation for Jane Hall's efforts to make her therapeutic efforts, "patient centered," acknowledging that rules need re-examining and that, "ONE SIZE DOES NOT FIT ALL" (her emphasis). Her presentation is mostly stripped of jargon, but I think we can go further in talking to each other in an experience-near manner, consistent with Hall's wish to level the field between patient and therapist so as to make the therapeutic dialogue one in which the patient is empowered to participate as the expert on what is in his/her mind and potentially enabled to identify how what's in their mind got there. I will quote selectively from Hall's chapter in considering the advantages, and potential pitfalls, of moving even further in a jargon-free direction.

In her introductory section, Hall suggests, "One common way to remain connected while at the same time separating, albeit in a compromised manner, is via identification with the aggressor." I would like to unpack this idea in my beginning attempt to illustrate what I have in mind. Describing human motivational states is complicated because motivation is complicated. Divergent aims are part and parcel of human behavior, which leads to the notion of "compromise formation." While our theories have leaned on this notion in reference to drive derivatives seeking expression, as well as to psychic defenses, the idea of compromise need not carry with it baggage from a particular metapsychological theory (e.g. drive theory). Hall is suggesting that for a child raised in a traumatic or abusive or neglectful environment there is often a need to find ways to both retain a needed attachment and to express rejection or hostility towards the attachment. "Identification with the aggressor" is a concept which suggests both (e.g. "I will take in my tormentor, emulate him/her, and dispense toward an other that to which I was subjected," complicated by the fact that the identification and the aggressive behavior are both determined unconsciously). This all makes sense to me, but I'm not sure how much the idea of "identification with the aggressor" adds to our work with patients. Using the concept is our own way of identifying with teachers, supervisors, authors, analysts who came before and letting each other know that we are from the same tribe. Clinically, I think the important principles are that we recognize a life-long need for and pursuit of attachment, and we recognize that relationship difficulties, including especially early difficulties with caretakers, make this a complicated pursuit.

As I wade into the interface between theory and the clinical setting which Hall presents, with her focus on patients whose sub-optimal early life experiences have contributed to chaotic experiences in relationships as they age, there is reference to "splitting," to the therapeutic task of translating action into words, to "strengthening the ego," and to regulating the patient's degree of regression. All of these concepts are familiar to analytic clinicians, but are they the most helpful way to describe what happens in the clinical setting? I choose these because of how commonplace they are, and my question/critique can apply to much of our usual use of clinical theory.

I'll start with the idea of splitting. The theory of defensive splitting comes from object relations thinking, with the notion that good images of self and other are kept separate from bad images so as to avoid catastrophic experiences of badness either attacking one from the inside or coming at one from bad others. Splitting is pictured as protecting a good sense of self or a benign experience of the other from these threats. OK, but I want to argue for the importance of recognizing that split states may arise from other than defensively motivated purposes. Extreme experiences of childhood overstimulation or abuse may be segmented off internally due to their extreme nature, not necessarily because it is too threatening to integrate them into one's encoded experiences of self or other. A patient's memory of being told by her beloved father that she is so much better than her peers is clung to because it carried with it a feeling of pride, goodness, superiority, a feeling of being loved most of all. Extreme affects lay down memory traces that preserve associated experiences and are not necessarily the result of "splitting." How do we tell in a given situation what gives rise to extreme, polarized portrayals of images of self/other and or to affective responses that are hard to account for because of their intensity? The answer, as it is in most (all?) clinical situations, is to remain curious without assuming that extremes of either/or represent defensiveness.

What about translating "actions into words"? Hall sees this happening when her patient, in a state of depression with vegetative symptoms is able to do the work of mourning and eventually to "say goodbye to a grandiose self" with the help of her therapy. Sometimes when therapists ask patients to put something they are enacting into words (facial grimaces, tears, hitting oneself or other versions of self-abuse), it comes across as if the therapist has a theory that action replaces words, and that maybe this replacement is defensively motivated, i.e. that it is too painful to entertain the words for what one is feeling. There is room for debate as to what extent psychoanalysis (or psychoanalytic therapy) is primarily a verbal form of treatment, in that much goes on, whether attended to or not, nonverbally. But there is something important about being able to put experience into words. Verbalizing a feeling requires being able to achieve sufficient distance from it, and sufficient perspective, to be able to capture the feeling in a manner that can be considered with another party. But I'm not sure that considering this movement from nonverbal to verbal is a "translation," and sometimes the preferred therapeutic movement is from just words to something felt that is beyond words. I think the back and forth between verbal and nonverbal is richer and more complicated than referring to it as translation makes it appear.

What about "strengthening the ego"? Late in his career, Charles Brenner moved away from the version of ego psychology to which he had been a major contributor. In positing that rather than seeing conflict as involving competing psychic structures, compromise involved competing trends within the psyche, e.g. experiences that arouse unpleasure might be warded off by more pleasurable content (see Brenner, C. (2006). If we are to look at psychic functions rather than reified psychic structures, we might be pressed to clarify what it is that we refer to as strengthening the ego. I have in mind such phrasing as building affect tolerance, increasing reflective capacity or mentalization, or loosening attachments to pain-inducing situations. While any of these could be seen as strengthening functions that structural theory assigned to the ego, perhaps we can let go of structural thinking, which I think is more experience-distant than the clinical situation deserves.

As for regulating regression, Hall tells us of a period of time when she and her patient met face-to-face, rather than the preferred use of the couch. She tells us, "I struggled with how much regression I thought we could and should tolerate. Sometimes we agreed that using the chair was preferable to the couch because looking at each other did serve to hold her together when fragmentation threatened." This interesting observation, connected to Hall's wish to help strengthen the patient's ego, can be thought about in different ways. Clearly, sitting up face-to-face changes the perspective and the stimuli most readily available for both parties. Being able to access the analyst's facial expressions may be a source of information that is lost with the lack of visual contact; the analyst's capacity to take in the patient's nonverbal responsiveness is increased relative to sitting outside the patient's sight with the patient in a prone position. This greater access of both parties may contribute to a less depriving (and therefore potentially less "fragmenting") atmosphere for patients, but is this more outer-directed than inner-directed connection necessarily less regressive? Perhaps it depends on the analyst-patient pair or on the stage of treatment; in any case, I'm not sure we are so much able to control the patient's degree of "regression," though we can surely provoke anxiety states or states of heightened affect by being more distant and depriving.

So, I'd like to encourage Hall to go further with her critique of certain traditional ways of viewing the clinical situation. I'd also like to encourage her to be more forceful in critiquing positions of authority in analytic work. I will select a few examples from her discussion to illustrate my points.

Hall tells us that when a patient is coming from a background where deprivation led to impaired capacity to trust, in the face of such lack of trust, "explanations and conversations work far better than interpretations with such patients." I am uncomfortable with the idea of giving patients explanations, though I certainly agree that we are trying to help them find explanations, and this task may be facilitated by tentatively offering a hypothesized explanation of our own. While I applaud Hall's wariness of interpretations given in a way that conveys the analyst's position of authority in relation to the dilemmas patients bring, does the idea of "explanation" move us away from such a position? Perhaps the crux of this lies in how one delivers one's comments, whatever we call them. What is involved in the search for explanation is really an alternative perspective. For example, a patient may assume

59

that he/she deserved to be treated abusively. Hall says that in such situations, "It is important to remember that what is familiar, no matter how painful, feels safe." We might approach such a patient with the perspective that they blame themselves because 1) they were blamed by others; 2) it gives them some feeling of both familiarity and control (if you were responsible, you could have avoided punishment by being better, and that idea is preferable to the idea that your caretakers were hateful or crazy or arbitrary in their punishment); 3) self-blame is intended to avoid the feared criticism coming at them from others. In the face of this dynamic, we offer the possibility of freeing themselves from extreme self-criticism, with the certainty that they need no longer fear abuse from others upon whom they are dependent.

The kind of explanation involved in bringing an outside perspective to patients' maladaptive formulations is arrived at slowly with much back and forth, so that it is truly a joint project. I imagine that Hall would agree with this and perhaps say that this is exactly what she said or implied. She says, "Food for thought is all we can give, but it is given with love." My point is that I think her saying that "explanations and conversations work far better than interpretations with such patients," implies a level of authority for the explanation-delivering analyst that in other places she is appropriately challenging.

One thing about the power of different perspectives being delivered in conversation is that this conforms with my understanding of building mentalization. In Fonagy's writings (e.g. Fonagy, 1995; Fonagy & Target, 1996; Target & Fonagy, 1996), the pre-stage of mentalizing is "psychic equivalence," which involves the conviction that what is in one's mind is what is real and therefore what is in everyone else's mind. The revelation in the context of a meaningful psychotherapy relationship that there are alternative ways to think about one's perceptions contributes to the strengthening of mentalization capacity.

Hall refers to the inability to mentalize as a box, akin to "borderline" into which we put patients such as her patient, Lois. A difference, though, is that the inability to mentalize is both something that is common to all of us under certain conditions (e.g. relationship stresses, anxiety states) and "borderline" is a designation that often implies "difficult to treat" and even "untreatable." Mentalization vulnerabilities are certainly treatable (though they may pose difficulties for the therapist).

Hall suggests: Try as we therapists do to compete with the bad enough object by offering ourselves as a new object, we sometimes fail and lose hope. This is understandable and not everyone is cut out for such difficult work. It is rarely gratifying and may even be considered as masochistic to try. So those who do hang in deserve appreciation.

At the end of the chapter, she suggests, "if we therapists are patient and courageous, connection can happen.... Two people take a journey during which new growth occurs and although the travel can be exhausting the rewards make it well worth it." I agree heartily with this statement. In my experience the work of connecting with someone with a problematic or abusive past can be extremely gratifying, and I don't think this experience is so rare. As I think about the course of my career, some of the most gratifying people to work with have also been those who struggle to form a connection. Upon further reflection, and with some fear that people who have not been so difficult to engage might feel slighted if they read this, I would say that every treatment has its potential gratifications for the therapist, but the slowly developing capacity to allow me to make mistakes (as happens inevitably) and then to still take in my observations/reflections is certainly a gratifying development in the treatment of those with limited initial capacity to mentalize.

So, I encourage Jane Hall to stay with the optimistic streak that runs through her chapter: change is possible for patents quite damaged by their early upbringings and participating in such change is gratifying to the therapist who does so. Techniques of working in such treatments can be described without resort to jargon, even to jargon that is so often used in our field as to be commonplace (dealing with "splitting," turning action into words, strengthening the "ego," monitoring regression, etc.). Two other phrases which Hall introduces are "self-murder" and "bad enough object" experience. I don't think either of these constructs helps her argument, and for me they detract.

I'll start with "self-murder;" I remember when I first became familiar with Shengold's *Soul Murder* (1989), to which Hall refers. I thought it was a terrific title, capturing the deadening effect on the adult internal world among those who suffered unspeakable abuse as youngsters. The people who commit such acts on children have problematic attitudes toward the children, highlighted by a hostility to the child's need to have his/her sense of self recognized and nurtured. This phenomenon is captured by the idea that they are engaged in interpersonal acts which kill off important elements of the child's self. Hall's self-murder is a related term. She tells us that it, "applies to self-states that reside in the whole self … [the term] is a literal way of saying that a cohesive self has not been achieved or that self and object differentiation has not occurred." It is observably the case that suicidal states of mind often include the wish to murder something inside, and this reflects a lack of realization that murder of one part of oneself is deadly for the whole self. It may be that that which one wishes to kill involves the internalization of an "other," or an "object" from one's earlier life. If this is what Hall has in mind, we are in agreement about the concept, but I don't find her terminology helpful. I would rather see a description of the nature of the depressive state, including elements of hopelessness and rage, which dominates the clinical picture.

Finally, does the "bad enough" construct help us in our work? It is useful to be reminded of Winnicott's notion of "good enough," but I think this idea was important as a reminder that one cannot, and should not, aim for perfection. Children, under optimal circumstances, grow from cycles of mistake and repair, as long as the loving, caring parent is able to stay present. I don't think there is an analog to "bad enough." I would say not good enough is bad. Period. We may shy away from saying that a certain mother or parent was "bad," and maybe "bad enough" is a tad less accusatory, but we need to be able to tune into patients' experiences of, and descriptions of, misalliance or insensitive or hostile parenting and recognize this as problematic or pathogenic.

For most of the 1990's I was the Director of a partial hospital program at Chestnut Lodge Hospital in Rockville, Maryland. I organized this program in response to the realization that many of the patients we saw with extreme Axis II difficulties did not need long-term hospitalization and even became more disorganized if treated in a confined setting. My work with staff and patients in the program was facilitated by my discovery of Peter Fonagy's papers on mentalization. Viewing our patients as struggling with mentalization vulnerabilities, rather than as defensively attacking members of staff, allowed staff to maintain greater empathy and to remain thoughtful in the face of hostility rather than becoming reactive. I think this is the essence of Hall's description of her work with Lois. Seeking to facilitate and sustain connection with disorganized patients is the therapist's task. It is what we strive for. To the extent that this has been a critique, it is not a critique of Hall's work but of how she talks about it. Leaving jargon, or theory, out of our descriptions to the extent possible can enrich our descriptions and invite conversation with our readers or listeners. This is to be desired.

References

Brenner, C. (2006). Psychoanalysis or Mind and Meaning. New York: *Psychoanalytic Quarterly.*

Fonagy, P. (1995). Playing With Reality: The Development of Psychic Reality and Its Malfunction in Borderline Personalities. *International Journal of Psychoanalysis,* 76: 39–44.

Fonagy, P. & Target, M. (1996). Playing With Reality: I. Theory of Mind and The Normal Development of Psychic Reality. *International Journal of Psychoanalysis,* 77: 217–233.

Shengold, L. (1989). *Soul Murder: The Effects of Childhood Abuse and Deprivation.* New Haven: Yale University Press.

Target, M. & Fonagy, P. (1996). Playing With Reality: II. The Development of Psychic Reality from A Theoretical Perspective. *International Journal of Psychoanalysis,* 77: 459–479.

"Self-Murder" and the Ignorant Psychoanalyst

Todd Dean

"**N**othing escapes from the writer's words, on the contrary, all things are hammered into them, annealed, fixed forever in rows and rows of the language he composes."

–Gilbert Sorrentino, *Splendide-Hôtel*, p. 26.

I very much appreciate Jane Hall's focus on the topic of this chapter: it has seemed to me for some time that, while psychoanalytic training has emphasized the importance of finding "analyzable" patients, the study of the unconscious is invaluable for working with the deeply traumatized. Perhaps more significant, from where I see it, is how much I have learned from working with such patients, which has come to seem to me much more than I could have learned from always working with the "analyzable" (a word that I believe must always be put in scare quotes, as Nabokov said of "reality").

That said, I do have some issues with the case as presented and the discussion that follows. These issues have mostly to do with what I would call the problematics of knowledge as it is presented in the paper: the problematics of knowing what is going on for the patient, yes, but, perhaps even more important, the problematics of knowing what is going on for the analyst. These are issues we are all dealing with every time we do analytic work.

I will start with the quotes Hall uses as epigrams for the book. The first is from Thomas Ogden: "The analyst's feeling of certainty is often tied to the idea that there exists a proper 'analytic technique'.... . By contrast, think of 'analytic style' as one's own personal creation that is loosely based on existing principles of analytic practice, but more importantly is a living process that has its origins in the personality and experience of the analyst". What struck me about this is the contrast Ogden makes between a seemingly objective, impersonal approach to the work, on the one hand, and the more personal process as developed by the analyst, on the other. I was struck by this way of thinking about the knowledge of the analyst in the work, that it is something that one can count on having, either through the objective, impersonal "technique" or the "living process". At least, there is no question of the role of knowledge in psychoanalytic work: the analyst must feel knowledgeable.

The second is from Rebecca Solnit, in which she states that "[t]oo many writers cannot come to terms with the ways in which the past, like the future, is dark.... . [T]here are limits to knowledge,... essential **mysteries**, starting with the notion that we know just what someone thought or felt in the absence of exact information". Solnit here is clear that we don't have the knowledge, but I was unclear if she was suggesting that there could be "exact information", but we couldn't count on getting it.

The final epigram is from a song by Peggy Lee, ending with the lines "I know a little bit about a lot of o' things /But I don't know enough about you". I appreciated this, because there is nothing to suggest that the knowledge the singer is lacking can be obtained: it's just not there, and there's no way of knowing that it will show up.

What concerns me is the implication, in Ogden's quote, at least, and in much of the clinical material Hall presents, that there is enough information to guarantee that we can know the truth, and from that, act accordingly. Reading through this, I found myself thinking about the book from which I have taken a quote as epigram, Gilbert Sorrentino's *Splendide-Hôtel*.

As I understand him, Sorrentino's point is that, whenever we try to speak truth, we are inevitably limited by our own words. There is *never* "enough information" to communicate or validate a truth. As one reader of Sorrentino has it, "Language is intentionally representational. It embodies our *intention* to represent extralinguistic reality. However, words inevitably replace the realities they intend to replicate, stand *in* for rather than stand for their referents. Distancing the 'facts' in this way, they defer our arrival at the epiphanies of truth they propose to facilitate. Language, therefore, is a system of representations that never succeeds in delivering what it promises. All we ever get is representations" (Mackey, p. 2). Mackey goes on: "[i]n the absence of an unmediated acquaintance with the represented, 'reality' and 'truth' designate selected groups of representations to which we ascribe the *authority* of truth and reality. Our selection of these 'authoritative' representations is not grounded in direct perception of fact: 'fact' itself is a mode of representation to which *factual status* has been selectively granted.... That we designate certain representations as 'factual' and 'truthful' is probably traceable to pragmatic causes. Some ways of imagining the world serve our purposes better than others, and for that reason we take them as veridical" (ibid.).

So, let's be real: if you are a psychoanalyst, you are ignorant. Period. But to be clear, I'm not saying this is a bad thing. In fact, as I hope to show, this is a good thing, and one that we need to emphasize.

The first time I was struck by this was during my analytic training, when we read the "Wolf Man" case. This was in the final semester of training at my institute, when the class read through several of Freud's case histories. Here Freud writes about the assumption that the Wolf Man saw his parents having sexual intercourse *a tergo*, and that "[i]t must therefore be left at this (I can see no other possibility): either the analysis based on the neurosis in his childhood is all a piece of nonsense from start to finish, or everything took place just as I have described it above" (p. 56). But he goes on to acknowledge that it didn't have to be that way: the Wolf Man grew up on a farm, and could have seen animals copulating thus, "which he then displaced on to his parents, as though he had inferred that his parents did things in the same way" (p. 57).

What blew me away about this was the question, why did Freud write all this out? How could he go from saying that, if his interpretation is to be construed as having any validity, there's no possibility that his patient didn't see his parents having sex in this way, to acknowledging how complicated things really are? Why didn't Freud just delete the insistence for which he "can see no other possibility" and explain what he came to see as the likely source for the Wolf Man's dream?

To be clear, I had become interested in psychoanalysis because what I was learning in "evidence-based" and "scientific" psychiatry was not impressing me very much: I was at the local institute to learn what mental health was really about, as opposed to checking boxes on the DSM-IIIR. Reading this passage in the case was troubling to me: if Freud realized what he had claimed was wrong, then why didn't he just delete the paragraphs in which he developed that argument, rather than go on to say, in effect, "oops"? By the time I had worked through this, though, I saw it very differently. This was my introduction to what makes Freud, in my mind, such an important thinker. His writing actually enacts the uncertainty that we are faced with in working with the unconscious, even though it seems clear to me that he would much rather things were more objectively clear, at least sometimes—like at the start of that paragraph about the Wolf Man's dream.

In the case of Lois, Hall clearly describes the complexities that psychoanalytic work can entail. When she writes, "So many things impinge on what we think of as normal development... all leaving cause and effect still mysterious... What appears as a normal family often hides chilling secrets", she is revealing a radical truth: we don't *know* what's going on, especially in a world that we think of as "normal". What is is communicated in language that is never—can never be—impartial and completely 'objective'.

That said, we must also accept that we can't be sure that what we, as analysts/therapists, are doing is also "right". To me, this means we always have to be thinking about the validity of our interventions and the understandings those interventions are based on. On this point, I agree with Hall re: the potential value of a different way of engaging a patient from what she describes as "the classical model of blank screen, neutral interpreter of conflict". However, I don't necessarily see what we are doing as an advance over other ways of doing the work. Instead, I would argue that we are in a unique situation *with everyone we work with,* and it is highly problematic to assume we are just employing a superior technique. Like the situation with Sorrentino's writer, the dyad's words are fixed in our language: we cannot claim an understanding beyond our words. In contrast to Hall's suggestion that analytic technique improves over time and with research, my sense is that over time analytic technique just can't stay the same. Again, we are ignorant.

But again, I'm not complaining about this. Being an ignorant psychoanalyst is not a bad thing. Freud's backing off of his certainty about what is happening in the Wolf Man's dream is a valuable part of his report of the case, because he is acknowledging, at least sort of, the mysteries inherent in being a psychoanalyst. Or, to quote Jacques Rancière's *The Ignorant Schoolmaster:* "...each of us describes our parabola around the truth. No two orbits are alike" (p. 59).

This is what the scholar Joseph Jacotot discovered, in 1818, when he was forced to teach French to Flemish students, after fleeing his native France because of the return of the Bourbon kings. He was given the chance to teach in the Netherlands, specifically, to teach French to students who only spoke a language he could not.

Without going into detail about this, I will note that, to Jacotot's surprise, the students were able to learn very well. Which was surprising to him, because the entire basis of education, as he understood it, was the ability of the teacher *to explain to the student*, which was definitely not what was happening here. This led to a whole new approach to thinking about education, one that had been minimized for a very long time but was explored by Rancière in the tumultuous aftermath of the protests of 1968.

Jacotot approached this seemingly impossible task not by trying to hold a position of mastery, but by focusing on "the *minimal link of a thing in common*" (p. 2) between himself and his students. He found this in a newly published bilingual edition of a French novel, and was puzzled by how well his students did: "How could these young people, *deprived of explanation*, understand and resolve the difficulties of a language entirely new to them?" (quoted, p. 2). In exploring this question, he came to realize that explaining things was of no benefit: in fact, explaining is a form of domination, "[a]nd this is why the explainers endanger our revolution" (p. 59).

If this is true for teaching a foreign language, it *has* to be true for the analytic process. In a very real way, I believe what Hall describes in this case illustrates that: she is not the master, applying the technique she learned in training to the case of Lois; rather, she is engaging with the analysand. My concern on this point is that she presents what she is doing as an advance over "classical" analytic technique, as though there is now a better form of explication for the analysand than there used to be. Instead, I would argue that her work is a place where analyst and analysand may come together and engage in the work they are doing. This, rather than any specific element of technique, is what brings value to our work.

But to be clear, it is a work that one will always have to think about and engage in. With every analysand, there will be places where our understanding is going to be off. E.g., where Hall writes "the contemporary therapist's calm respectful stance is often the first experience of concern for some patients," I was reminded of a patient who had suffered years of sexual abuse as a child by a family acquaintance, but who, when she started seeing me, had no memory of this fact. It was only years into the treatment, during which I was always trying to give her a space in which to say what mattered to her, that she finally was able to tell me that my "calm, respectful stance" reminded her of how her abuser never spoke when he was abusing her. I felt terrible when I heard this, but also, on reflection, I realized that this was just the way this had to be worked out: even if I had, somehow, intuited what she told me long before she put it into words, it would almost certainly have been a meaningless intervention: she had to get to where she could verbalize what she felt, herself.

The issue here is not just my ignorance. It is also spoken to in what Sorrentino describes: words don't give us actuality, The Truth. In our work, actuality has to *arrive:* it was deferred action, not interpretation/construction/explanation/conversation—it was not me bringing the actual into the discussion, that had this effect. As Maurice Blanchot puts it, in *The Writing of the Disaster:* "The disaster ruins everything, all the while leaving everything intact. It does not touch anyone in particular; 'I' am not threatened by it, but spared, left aside. It is in this way that I am threatened.... Thus, the disaster is always being minimized and 'normalized'" (Blanchot, p. 2). A Bosnian refugee once described to me an example of this: "It is not normal, but it was normal to see dead bodies, exploded limbs...". The most horrific experiences become normal, and we can't just interpret them away.

I appreciate Hall's thoughtfulness and willingness to move outside a prescribed way of doing our work (wherever that prescription came from). I just want to be clear that we cannot speak of "progress" in our work: we will always have to be open, thoughtful, engaged—and ignorant.

In short, psychoanalysis really is an impossible profession, like teaching and government. Assuming an empirical advance in the field will never not be problematic, because it implies mastery by the analyst, which is an impossibility. But again, this impossibility is, I believe, an unambiguously good thing: the work we do is for the liberation of the subject, and for that to happen, mastery, expertise, *knowledge* itself, are problems. Getting at truth is something we must approach very humbly.

References

Blanchot, M (1980/1995). *The Writing of the Disaster,* translator A. Smock. Lincoln and London, University of Nebraska Press.

Freud, S. (1918). "From the History of an Infantile Neurosis" *S. E.* XVII, pp. 3–123.

Mackey, L. (1997). *Fact, Fiction, and Representation: Four Novels by Gilbert Sorrentino.* Camden House, Columbia, SC.

Rancière, J. (1969/91*). The Ignorant Schoolmaster: Five Lessons in Intellectual Emancipation,* trans. Kristin Ross. Stanford UP, Stanford, CA.

Sorrentino, G. (1973, 1984). *Splendide-Hotel.* Dalkey Archive Press, Elmwood Park, IL.

On Introducing Hockey Sticks into a Soccer Match—Response to Jane Hall's Chapter 8: "What Happens in Psychoanalytic Treatment? What's it All About?"

Francisco Somarriva Pinto

Answering 'What happens in psychoanalytic treatment?' is a daring task. This question relates to pointing out the essence of psychoanalysis and psychoanalytic experience, which may lead us to a Platonic discussion similar to answering what makes a chair a chair. What are the necessary and sufficient elements and phenomena a treatment must have to be called 'psychoanalytic'? What phenomena may transform a psychotherapeutic approach into a 'non-psychoanalytic' one? Is a psychoanalytic treatment defined by its structuring elements, purpose, or aims, if any? Is it possible to separate them? Interrogating these topics usually causes division among psychoanalysts, who sometimes engage in heated discussions on how many carats their psychoanalytic gold has. As the jokes say, where there are two psychoanalysts, there are three different ideas, and where there are two Lacanian psychoanalysts, there are three different psychoanalytic training institutes.

After reading her book chapter, I first thought Hall offered a condensed version of her clinical and theoretical views about psychoanalytic treatment, aiming to engage different audiences and connect with them. Then, I reflected on her psychoanalytic training journey, imagining that it was inaugurated by teachings in classical psychoanalysis and her first analysis, then continued through relational psychoanalysis and her second analysis, and now is currently addressing neurosciences. Her journey also seemed to cover object relations theory (Klein, 1946), the importance of real traumatic events during childhood (Ferenczi, 1916–1917), and life trajectories theory. This journey is reflected in her *teasing apart and integrating theoretical understandings'* when answering what a psychoanalytic treatment is, which was narrated as if she was free-associating, going back and forth on complex topics such as therapeutic goals, the psychoanalytic frame, therapeutic alliance, deprivation, mental growth, and emotional experiences in the analytic situation. I was left with the idea that Hall tried to house many topics in her answer, showing her experiences as a psychoanalyst and the wide variety of phenomena that take place during a psychoanalytic treatment.

However, during my reading of her work, I perceived Hall abruptly and consistently changing frameworks during her exposition. I felt myself constantly and swiftly jumping from one theoretical and technical approach to another while following her description of what happens during psychoanalytic therapy. For example, on one occasion, she moved from respecting the role of early defenses in diminishing shame, passing by the internalization of the analyst, to referring to oxytocin's role in positive and erotic transference. Would this have occurred because the author was writing for in-depth psychotherapists as stated in her introduction, and assumed they could follow her? As a traveler, I got dizzy, like when you are in the back seat of a car driving through a downhill slope full of curves.

While trying to understand this sensation, I remembered the words of my first psychoanalytic supervisor. Similar to what Hall mentioned about finding your own analytic voice and ears, Coloma (2011) said psychoanalysts need to rigorously train and study in-depth the theoretical and clinical approaches they want to use to inform their free-floating listening. Only in that way, he said, psychoanalysts would be able to use psychoanalytic authors 'incorrectly'—they would be free to use different theories beyond their original purpose, as they know their boundaries and elasticity. In my own words, psychoanalytic training and practice mean learning the different ways of playing with psychoanalysis, thoroughly understanding and experiencing the game rules and dynamics of each theory and clinical approach an analyst wants to play with. Doing so would allow analysts to teach their patients how to play and play with them, eventually leading to a way of playing in which the participants can play freely without focusing on how to play. As Hall says, their playing together, their relationship, has become part of themselves.

Nonetheless, unlike the author, Coloma added a precaution: analysts should be coherent and consistent in their listening and understanding of their patients, as the analyst's jumping from one theoretical and clinical framework to another during a session or a treatment may risk using two or more conflicting and opposite clinical interventions and thus cause confusion in the patient's mind. Using the 'playing a game' metaphor, analysts and patients might get confused during treatment if the game, either its rules or essence, suddenly changes because an analyst introduces elements from a different game, attempts to change a rule while playing, or overwhelms the players by playing different games simultaneously. For example, you do not introduce hockey sticks in the middle of a soccer match (or football, as the rest of the world outside the United States calls it), as this action may confuse the players.

To illustrate how this confusion may affect psychoanalytic treatment, allow me to briefly discuss the concept of countertransference. After the inaugural 'analyst's need for more analysis' understanding of this unconscious experience by Freud (1910), which was also sustained by Klein (Spillius, 2007) and expanded by Winnicott (1949b), Paula Heimann (1950) revolutionized psychoanalytic practice by saying that countertransference refers to the emotions felt by the analyst, thus creating a plethora of different approaches to this clinical phenomenon (Racker, 1969). That is to say, she opened the door for many analysts to explore different ways of playing with this concept. Just considering two of them for this exposition, one states that countertransference refers to the analyst's feelings resulting from their analysand's projection of their feelings into them (Carpy, 1989), and the other defined it as the emotional expression of the analyst's digestion of the unconscious elements projected by the analysand (Bion, 1959; Rosenfeld, 1971). Depending on which one an analyst chooses, their way of creating interpretations and their theories of the mind are deeply impacted.

I have found that Heimann's understanding of countertransference is predominant in many psychoanalytic regions and schools. One of the clearest examples of the prevalence of this view occurs when a supervisor, discussants, or audience members ask during a case presentation, *'What is your countertransference?'* To me, this is an impossible question to answer on the spot. How can I or anyone be aware or conscious of an unconscious experience? Following Bollas (1983), as countertransference is truly an unconscious phenomenon, it may take months or even years to be understood. Thus, creating countertransference-informed interventions while taking the latter approach can only be done *a posteriori*. Moreover, until supervision, self-analysis, and/or the analyst's work on the analysand's material transforms the analyst's countertransference into something thinkable, there is little to no possibility of creating interventions that can be used in the same session that a countertransferential phenomenon occurs, which is the opposite of Heimann's and related proposals. While an analyst who chooses to understand countertransference following Bollas's definition would create and time their interpretations at a slower pace compared to the "what I feel is what the patient feels" approach, it would also grant them time to reflect and digest their emotional experience in such a way that the risk of confusing their unconscious conflicts with their emotional reactions and countertransferential manifestations in their mind would be greatly reduced.

With all this in mind, I would like to offer the reader a statement: if an analyst suddenly changes their theoretical framework in the middle of a session, whether due to their countertransferential enactment or a clinical decision detached from their patient's material, it will produce a domino effect on how they listen to the material, experience their emotions, create interpretations, and see their patients. Therefore, using different understandings and techniques that greatly change the configuration of the analytic situation risks introducing confusion in the analytic relationship with the patient—it is akin to suddenly introducing hockey sticks into a soccer match without noticing it.

Hall's case presentation of Donna may be a good example of this. The author's view of her patient at times is closer to the Freudian understanding of a neurotic patient and to what Lacanians would call the 'Subject of the Other' (Etchegoyen, 2005), who reenacts the repressed unconscious and brings it to their therapeutic relationship or 'the analysis' through the transference. This happened when she directed her undigested rage toward her analyst. At other times, Donna is a patient whose growth is measured in terms of Ego strength and adaptation (Nunberg, 1942). Hall sees her loss of jobs and opportunities as an attack on her progress and the analysis. As the author pointed out, the analyst she described had at least three possible ways to understand Donna's negative transference, discussing three different clinical ways to work with it. By trying to step out of the transference, I understand that the analyst offered Donna a way to differentiate her transference from her 'real' analyst, trying to use her Ego strength to help Donna think about what was going on between them. Paraphrasing what she wrote, I believe the analyst said implicitly, 'I do not want to be your mother, so let us think about what is going on here. Transference happens, but sometimes it is not helpful.' On the one hand, in my view, the analyst offered Donna a devaluation of her transference (by using a suggestive intervention?), strengthening her Ego and aligning her with what the analyst and the patient consider success. Moreover, the analyst then identified with her client's experience of losing a good object. On the other hand, it was unclear why the analyst had difficulties tolerating Donna's anger, especially after stating that they could contain it before. Again, I got confused. Maybe I missed something?

Soon after re-reading her presentation, I began to wonder what Hall meant by progress in Donna's life and why the author considered her patient was sabotaging it. If Donna's loss of jobs and opportunities were understood as sabotage to progress, would psychoanalytic progress be measured by getting a job? Or is the emergence of rage and destruction a sign of progress? According to Hall's view of what happens in psychoanalytic treatment, it could be both. I also saw inconsistencies in the author's therapeutic approach when offering the interpretation, I paraphrased above. The analyst offered themselves as a good object so that Donna could incorporate their attitude *"alongside the troubling mother representation,"* which Hall saw as a corrective experience. However, explicitly telling Donna not to engage in her negative transference because it was not helpful could also be understood as the analyst enacting her countertransference. I think that the analyst may have unconsciously invited Donna to be a good girl again, offering her a way to win her analyst's love (hockey stick) by letting go of her transferential rage (soccer match), thus confirming that being a good daughter will keep her mother's goodness alive[1]. What kind of analyst did Donna internalize? If negative transference is sometimes not helpful,

---

[1]Maybe her mother's depression relates to Andre Green' dead mother (1983) and Donna has to keep her alive someway.

does the same apply to negative countertransference? Could encouraging Donna to be a good girl be called progress? Or would it be sabotage?

Donna's case brought Hall's question in the introduction of this book about negative transference back to my mind: how much and how long it needs to be expressed. To whom is negative transference not always helpful to be expressed, the patient or the analyst? I think we as psychoanalysts need to be capable of distinguishing between the unconscious dynamics during a session and the frustration of not being a good analyst (Stein, 1991) in order to be able to offer patients what they need. Would this be something that distinguishes psychoanalytic treatment from other forms of therapy?

Along with this observation, it might be worth asking whether an analyst risks too much by attempting to offer a corrective experience, if such a thing exists, because of the possibility of becoming blind to their own wishes to be good to their patients. Much has been written about this critique (Knight, 2005; Christian et al., 2012; Aron et al., 2018). Can an analyst presenting themselves as a good object truly provide a corrective experience if it does not allow the (negative) transference to unfold? Hall's understanding of this psychoanalytic concept shows that an analyst can be internalized alongside the internal parental figures without replacing them, creating *"different brain pathways that exist alongside [...] the old ones,"* which sounds more like a creative process than a corrective one. Then, what is a corrective experience? Is it the creation of new brain pathways, the re-transcription of memories, or both?

Returning to Hall's case studies, her second one, Bill, was trickier for me. I had difficulty grasping what was psychoanalytic about it. This brief vignette summarized Bill's life, his second analysis attempt with a female analyst, and how being listened to and repairing trust helped him change. However, I could not find what the analyst said or did besides the aforementioned actions—no soccer ball, no hockey sticks even.

Although it could be said that the analyst's listening was psychoanalytic, as she was able to recognize that being a woman might be sensitive to Bill because of his past relationship with his mother, I struggled to find what was specifically psychoanalytic about Bill's treatment compared to what other psychotherapies might offer him, as there were no examples of the role of the analyst in this vignette. Furthermore, clinicians using other approaches such as Jungian psychology, systemic therapy, and the recently rebranded object-relations-informed practice called 'Internal Family Systems' could have reached a similar conclusion about the role of Bill's parents in his development. Is Hall's concept of development re-railing a structural characteristic of a psychoanalytic treatment exclusively?

In my experience, psychoanalysis is not the privileged device in which patients may express their intense feelings, rebuild their trust in others, or re-rail development, nor is it the only available therapeutic approach that may offer a space for these experiences to take place. Many patients readily bring their feelings to a session, not because of their treatments' effectiveness, frame, or progression, but as part of their transference and the complexity of their psychic and social conflicts. Can we consider the patient's emotional expression as evidence of the unfolding of psychoanalytic treatment, as Hall suggested at the beginning of her chapter? Ferenczi (1909) proposed that positive and negative transferences emerge from the patient's spontaneous psychic work, which the analyst might not have caused. Sometimes, we are just there, witnessing it take place, being the audience to an already written script, no matter how we are seated in our armchairs. For this reason, it is hard for me to conceive that the emotional expression of patients is always and necessarily linked to the progression of treatment.

Then again, what distinguishes psychoanalytic treatment from all other treatment modalities? Hall, for example, mentioned that psychoanalytic treatment differs from Cognitive Behavioral Therapy (CBT) in terms of their long-term outcomes, which left me wanting to hear more thoughts on it. Thinking about these differences made me reflect on my own experiences with CBT. In a seminar I had to attend, one participant asked the fairly known CBT therapist giving the seminar, 'What do you do if a patient brings you a dream to a session?' This clinician replied:

> *I once had a woman who came to treatment and brought a dream to the session. She told me about her dream, and I proceeded to work on the dream in a CBT way, asking questions about intermediate thoughts, cognitive distortions, and core beliefs. We talked about it on that day, and she never brought a dream again to her treatment. You see, long ago, I was talking to a psychoanalyst, and he told me that, in a way, psychoanalysts do CBT sometimes as they can also do those kinds of interventions. I told him that he was wrong, as he was not making CBT interventions as he was not thinking in a CBT way in his mind.*

I think the CBT clinician had a point. Psychotherapy theories and practices, such as psychoanalysis, mostly live in a therapist's mind, in their inner mental frame (Coloma, 2011). Moreover, psychoanalysis is a way of understanding the world and our psychic lives, a way of thinking, and a way of playing. Free association is one of the game rules that makes the psychoanalytic treatment experience possible, requiring the patient to speak their mind and the analyst to be ready and willing to hear everything they say[2]. I think Hall correctly described many daily-life experiences that psychoanalysis can listen to: *"thoughts, feelings, dreams, wishes, fears, ideas, beliefs, opinions, [...] expressed both in actions and words, both consciously and unconsciously."* I would add jokes, Freudian slips, fashion, music, and art. An analyst not only wants to listen to these experiences but also analyze

---

[2]One may wonder if the analyst can truly listen to everything the patient says and the limits of free association, but that is a discussion for a different time.

them, meaning finding out the hidden or buried painful truth condensed in them or building meaning where there has not even been one. Through this process, what the patient cannot remember is enacted in the transference.

Having this in mind, I posit that free association is one structural element that significantly distinguishes psychoanalytic treatment from the rest, as it allows patients and analysts, following Hall's metaphor, to embark as travelers in the unknown territories of the transitional space created by the establishment of a relationship between them. Differently from the CBT therapist mentioned above, the participants of a psychoanalytic treatment create their journey as they travel through it. Alternatively, using Freudian language, psychoanalysis collects the pieces of the long-forgotten, broken, or intact artifacts while unveiling and unburying them (Freud, 1937). Also, given the manualized nature of CBT and other therapies, my experience has been that what the patient says tends to be saturated with meaning by the therapist, thereby communicating to the former that there are expectations of what to say and bring to the latter. Thus, the CBT therapist's inner frame is filled with meaning, a plan, and goals—they already know how and where to go. Using Hall's metaphor, the CBT therapist guides the patient through a path already written, where little to no deviations are permitted. Thus, a dream is no longer owned by the patient but by the therapist. The therapist owns the ball and the game, and the players can only play it in one way, a rigid way. No wonder their patient stopped bringing dreams.

At this moment in this article, I feel compelled to clarify that I do not have a particular love for rules. I think Hall was right about moving away from authoritative, rigid, and orthodox psychoanalysis and creating her own 'slang.' However, I believe that creating and practicing your singular psychoanalytic style, as the author did, requires minimal conditions for it to exist, grow, and thrive. I see the psychoanalytic frame, particularly the rule of free association, as the supporting structure that allows travelers to embark on a journey and analysts and patients to play within the analytic situation. I think the living process that Ogden and Hall propose can only happen with this scaffolding underneath. What is the rule of free association but an invitation to play freely with the analyst? What is transference but the installation of a forced game within the therapeutic relationship, in which the analyst is pressured to play a role the patient unconsciously expects? As Bleger (1967) states, one of the first signs of resistance and transference in analysis is when the patient attempts and/or disrupts the frame, as their psychopathology installs itself within it. He also suggested that a sign of the analyst's enactment of their countertransference is when they disrupt the frame. For this reason, we analysts have to be extremely careful not to change the analytic contract by freely introducing our games and toys (hockey sticks) into the playing that the patient unconsciously proposes (soccer match), whether for loving theory, morality, or wanting to be good objects. Patients already have to bear with our poorly (and much needed by them) embodying and giving life to the characters in their unconscious script.

Finally, I would like to conclude this paper by adding a few observations to Hall's chapter. Even though it is clear to me that Hall's inner frame is psychoanalytical, I believe it loses its richness when theories such as neurosciences and early traumatic experiences are included in her chapter. On the one hand, I share the author's interest in neurosciences and would suggest the reader explore the remarkable work of Mark Solms on bridging it with psychoanalysis (Solms & Lechevalier, 2002; Solms, 2013). Nevertheless, Hall's way of presenting the relationship between mind and body tends to be superficial and diminishes the value of symbol formation, as she mostly focuses on the brain. This has been most interesting to me culturally, as I have noticed that people in the United States in their daily lives mostly use the word 'brain' instead of 'head' or 'mind' to refer to the place where thoughts or mental processes occur. I believe Winnicott (1949a) was right when he proposed that the mind is not located in the brain, head, or any specific part of our bodies, given that our body representation is a construction strongly determined by our psychosexual development, unconscious fantasies, and early experiences (Doltó, 2023). In Freud's (1888) words, *"hysteria behaves as though anatomy did not exist or as though it had no knowledge of it"* (pp. 169). Ultimately, our experiences of our bodies will always be a construction despite the several brain and bodily processes involved. This is even more critical if we consider that it was recently discovered that memory and learning processes might not only occur in neural cells (Kukushkin et al., 2024). Because of this, I believe we are still very far from fully understanding the role of our bodies, including the brain, in our psychic processes, leading me to leave this topic to the experts. This is a soccer match I do not dare to join yet.

On the other hand, I appreciate that Hall is clear about the kind of patients and psychoanalytic work she has been doing over these past years, focusing on those travelers who have experienced deprivation from their caretakers during childhood and basing her work on the analytic dyad and getting development back on track. However, I have two remarks about the author's approach. First, many of our patients do not necessarily have experienced trauma during their childhood. Sometimes, psychotic children are born within well-enough families. Other times, there are events outside the scope of the caregivers, such as chronic diseases or acute illnesses, that deeply affect them during early childhood and leave their caregivers powerless. As Winnicott (1965) said, *"It makes no difference if it was something in the parents that caused the child's illness. Often this is the case. But the damage was done neither willfully nor wantonly. It just happened"* (pp. 68). On top of that, there is also a type of patient that may unconsciously use their traumatic experiences, although true and justified, as part of their secondary gain narratives. This topic is a tremendous clinical challenge and leads us to the land of sadomasochism. Psychoanalytic treatment is perhaps the only clinical device that gives space to these clinical phenomena today, and it does not have too much room in Mahler's approach and, therefore, in Hall's view.

My second remark concerns the analytic dyad. My argument does not involve establishing the number of individuals or objects present during early infancy, which could lead to an endless discussion about pre-oedipal and oedipal experiences during the first years of life. Instead, I would like to point out that the analytic dyad exists within a third space, a transitional space (Winnicott, 1951), the place of playing and culture. This critique of the lack of mention of cultural structures in Mahler's separation-individuation theory is not new (Chodorow, 1978). I only found a few references in Hall's chapters given to me to read about the role that United States society, politics, and cultural nuances play in psychoanalytic treatment, which was mostly described in a catastrophic and anxiety-provoking way. Although there is some truth in how she views them, I believe her exposition loses richness by not including how culture supports and sometimes invades psychoanalytic treatment. I believe the analyst has a role in keeping hope that there is a world where we can all live, belong, and change (if we want to), which the caregivers transmit to their children as they grow in independence and autonomy. For this reason, adding the cultural environment surrounding psychoanalytic treatment to her views would enrich the author's exposition.

References

Aron, L., Grand, S., & Slochower, J. A. (Eds.). (2018). *De-idealizing Relational Theory: A Critique from Within.* Routledge.

Bleger, J. (1967). Psicoanálisis del encuadre psicoanalítico. *Revista de Psicoanálisis,* 24(2), pp.241–258.

Bion, W. R. (1959). Attacks on linking. *The International Journal of Psychoanalysis,* 40, pp.308–315.

Bollas, C. (1983). Expressive Uses of the Countertransference—Notes to the Patient from Oneself. *Contemporary Psychoanalysis*, 19, pp.1–33.

Carpy, D. (1989). *Tolerando la Contratransferencia: Un Proceso Mutativo*. Libro Anual de Psicoanálisis, 5, pp.233–240.

Chodorow, N. (1978). *The Reproduction of Mothering: Psychoanalysis and the Sociology of Gender*. University of California Press.

Doltó, F. (2023). *The Unconscious Body Image*. (S. Bailly Trans.). Routledge. (Original work published in 1984).

Coloma, J. (2011). *El Oficio en lo Invisible. Los Derechos del Paciente en la Práctica Psicoanalítica*. Santiago, Chile: Editorial Ocho Libros.

Christian, C., Safran, J. D., & Muran, J. C. (2012). The Corrective Emotional Experience: A Relational Perspective and Critique. In Castonguay, L.G., Hill, C.E. (Eds.) *Transformation in Psychotherapy* (pp.51–67). APA Books.

Etchegoyen, H. (2005). *Los Fundamentos de la Técnica Psicoanalítica* (2nd Edition). Buenos Aires, Argentina: Amorrortu Editores.

Ferenczi, S. (1909). Introjection and Transference. In Rickman, J. (Eds.) *First Contributions to Psychoanalysis* (pp.35–93). London: Karnac.

———— (1916–1917). Disease- or Patho-neuroses. In Rickman, J. (Eds.) *Further Contributions to the Theory and Technique of Psychoanalysis* (pp.78–88). London: Karnac.

Freud, S. (1888). Some Points for a Comparative Study of Organic and Hysterical Motor Paralyses. In *The Revised Standard Edition of the Complete Psychological Works of Sigmund Freud*, Volume I, pp.183–199. London, UK: Rowman & Littlefield Lanham, MD., The Institute of Psychoanalysis.

———— (1910). The Future Prospects of Psychoanalytic Therapy. In *The Revised Standard Edition of the Complete Psychological Works of Sigmund Freud,* Volume XI, pp.125–148. London, UK: Rowman & Littlefield Lanham, MD., The Institute of Psychoanalysis.

———— (1937). Constructions in Analysis. In *The Revised Standard Edition of the Complete Psychological Works of Sigmund Freud,* Volume XXIII, pp.237–258. London, UK: Rowman & Littlefield Lanham, MD., The Institute of Psychoanalysis.

Green, A. (1983). The Dead Mother. In A. Green. (1986). *On Private Madness.* Madison, CT: International Universities Press.

Heimann, P. (1950). On Countertransference. *The International Journal of Psycho-Analysis,* 31, pp.81–84.

Klein, M. (1946). Notes on Some Schizoid Mechanisms. *International Journal of Psychoanalysis,* 27, pp.99–110.

Knight, Z. G. (2005). The Use of the 'Corrective Emotional Experience' and the Search for the Bad Object in Psychotherapy. *American Journal of Psychotherapy, 59*(1), pp.30–41.

Kukushkin, N. V., Carney, R. E., Tabassum, T., & Carew, T. J. (2024). The Massed-spaced Learning Effect in Non-neural Human Cells. *Nature Communications, 15*(1), p.9635.

Nunberg, H. (1942). Ego Strength and Ego Weakness. *American Imago,* 3, pp.25–40.

Racker, H. (1969). La Contratransferencia. En *Estudios sobre Técnica Psicoanalítica,* pp:68–78. Buenos Aires: Editorial Paidós.

Rosenfeld, H. (1971). Contribution to the Psychopathology of Psychotic States: The Importance of Projective Identification in the Ego Structure and the Object Relations of the Psychotic Patient. In Doucet, P. & Laurin C. (Eds.) *Problems of Psychosis*, (pp.115–128). La Hague: Excerpta Medica.

Solms, M. (2013). Preliminaries for an integration of psycho-analysis and neuroscience. In *The Annual of Psychoanalysis*, 28, pp.179–200. London: Routledge.

———— & Lechevalier, B. (2002). Neurosciences and Psychoanalysis. *The International Journal of Psychoanalysis*, 83(1), pp.233–237.

Spillius, E. (2007). *Encounters with Melanie Klein. Selected Papers of Elizabeth Spillius*. The New Library of Psychoanalysis. London: Routledge.

Stein, S. (1991). La Influencia de la Teoría en la Contratransferencia del Psicoanalista. *Libro Anual de Psicoanálisis*, 7, pp.109–118.

Winnicott, D. W. (1949a). Chapter XIX. Mind and its Relation to the Psyche-Soma. In Winnicott, D.W. (1975) *Through Paediatrics to Psycho-Analysis* (pp.243–254). The International Psycho-Analytical Library.

———— (1949b). Hate in Counter-Transference. *The International Journal of Psycho-Analysis,* 30, pp.69–74.

———— (1951). Chapter XVIII. Transitional Objects and Transitional Phenomena. In Winnicott, D.W. (1975) *Through Paediatrics to Psycho-Analysis* (pp.229–242). The International Psycho-Analytical Library.

———— (1965). The Effect of Psychosis on Family Life. In L. Cadwell & H. Taylor Robinson (Eds.) *The Collected Works of D. W. Winnicott. Volume 6.* (pp.65–72). New York, United States: Oxford University Press.

Transformative Conversations On "What Happens in a Psychoanalytic Treatment? What is it All About?"

Fred Gioia

After reading chapter 8 of her latest book, titled "What Happens in Psychoanalytic Treatment? What's it All About" I found Jane Hall's ideas resonant with my own work with patients and with a contemporary neuro-psychoanalytic understanding of therapeutic models of change. Hall credits Norman Doidge's book "The Brain That Changes Itself" for providing the neuro-scientific foundation to her ideas.

As Hall's book seems geared towards professionals and those not as familiar with psychoanalysis, she begins the chapter revisiting central tenets of psychoanalysis. Hall outlines how developmental trauma is internalized and acted out as adults in a maladaptive fashion. What may have been necessary or useful as a child, no longer functions for the patient in an adaptive way. It is these limited emotional/relational repertoires that underly the psychological pain that bring folks into therapy.

Hall elegantly summarizes the transformative value of a psychoanalytic treatment as: "Perceptions that had been black and white and one dimensional expand into colorful multidi-mensionality." In essence, treatment she says, births an open-ness to alternative possibilities that expand upon the limited set of priors based on earlier experience. She elaborates the mechanism whereby "different brain pathways exist along the side of the old ones." This idea is consistent with current neuro-psychoanalytic thinking of therapeutic change which cites that as more effective means of navigating emotional conflicts are discovered, less psychological energy is needed to bolster defenses.

Jane Hall identifies the fear of change and stepping outside one's comfort zone as the roadblock to incorporating the in-sight that is gained in a psychoanalytic psychotherapy. Most importantly, she stresses the connection between the two people in the room, the patient and the therapist, as the prin-cipal catalyst to bring about such change i.e., to rework the old and create something new. This, in a sense, helps devel-opment get back on track.

Hall keenly points out the double-edged nature of psychoan-alytic work which both fosters a dependency and needed con-nection alongside promotion of self-sufficiency. Untangling these two and seeing that they are not "oil and water" ap-pears to be a central part of therapeutic work. Hall goes on to reiterate the psychoanalytic directive of bringing what was once unconscious into awareness through enactments in the transference. The pain that accompanies the prior maladap-tive solutions can be dissipated via a co-created reparative process that takes place within the analytic dyad.

I do have one disagreement with Hall when she speaks about how reality changes with growth. Perhaps this is semantics, but I don't see that it is reality that changes, but rather our predictions about it change as we develop. I think it would be more apt to say our internalized model of the world changes as we grow. A $5 bill takes on new meaning to an adolescent vs. a toddler. This is not because a bill has changed in reality, but rather the internalized model of how an adolescent sees the bill has changed.

Nevertheless, her conclusion remains consistent with modern therapeutic approaches in that there is a need to address the patient with an approach commensurate with their level of developmental trauma e.g. a highly empathic approach with those who have suffered 'soul murder' from caregivers at an early age. Hall acknowledges that "independence is not always realized" in a psychoanalytic psychotherapy "due to one's pull towards the safety of the familiar." But that on some level, "the past gets revised due to fresh perception." She continues that this revision is mediated by the relationship with the analyst whose benign curiosity fosters an atmosphere of recognition to allow exploration of past trauma, and, ultimately, address distorted ideas that the patient holds about themselves.

Halls thesis is best encapsulated with her emphasis on therapeutic action occurring within a *'conversation'*, where intimate ideas are exchanged with a non-critical empathically attuned adult. Hall argues that many have not experienced such a vulnerable and growth promoting interaction in their development. Her conception is simple and speaks to what I see as a fundamental relational truth about a healthy and effective therapeutic relationship. A *conversation* offers a critical pathway for human connection as well as how we learn from each other.

I do wish she would have stretched the idea of *'conversation'* a bit farther to include any type of deep relating within a dyad where there is empathic attunement and a desire to understand and exchange information with the other. In my view this does not necessarily require spoken words, although spoken language tends to be given a preeminent status in a psychoanalytic therapy. In this context, the spirit of her thesis still holds, that is relationships, good enough or not, are a principal medium in which all of us develop our sense of self and the world around us. Healthy ones can therefore be utilized in the service of learning how to help oneself.

Hall provides two brief vignettes to bolster her ideas. In one she tells of a woman, Donna, who struggles with a problematic maternal transference towards her analyst. An important *conversation* occurs when the therapist confronts Donna, stating that *something* is happening between them given Donna's resistance to incorporating the therapeutic work in her life. Donna responds desperately and angrily that the therapist isn't able to help her get better. The analyst confronts her stating that Donna is relating to her as if she were her presumptuous mother. This comment interrupts Donna's transferential spell, affording Donna the ability to see that she is motivated to defeat the analysis in a deleterious attempt to not lose the analyst. In a moment of disclosure, the analyst responds that perhaps Donna can keep her *in mind* even when they are not together, as the analyst did with her own analyst.

Although implied in the chapter, Hall's presentation of *conversation* between patient and analyst is not a one-way mirror, but one that requires vulnerability and disclosure from all parties. Not only is the transference called to attention, but the analyst reveals her own humanness in her response; that she too has had to struggle with the loss of an important person in her life. The analyst shares her strategy of attenuating the pain of loss by maintaining a mental *conversation* with her own analyst. Whether or not Donna takes up this strategy may not be the point, rather, the point being that there is a means of working through loss. There are possibilities beyond being stuck in the same self-defeating cycle.

Hall shares another vignette about a wounded man, Bill, who internalized an abusive and abandoning father figure. His identification with distorted aspects of masculinity resulted in an estrangement from familial relationships and ultimately himself. Bill only learned to tolerate his own shame of feeling defeated and weak through the relationship with an analyst. The analyst was able to contain Bill's anger and disdain, while remaining empathically attuned. As a result of these ongoing *conversations*, Bill's 'soldierly façade melted'. The point Hall makes is that through a corrective relational experience, unconscious distorted patterns can be illuminated, and newer, more adaptive ways of relating can be promoted within the dyad.

In her chapter on "What Happens in Psychoanalytic Treatment? What's it All About?" Jane Hall shares her wisdom of five decades in the field as a psychoanalyst. In doing so she provides a roadmap of what a successful psychoanalytic therapy can look like. When one strips away certain theoretical language, what comes to the foreground is a simple idea, one of an authentic *conversation*. Hall stresses the idea that the analytic setting affords a space for non-critical listening and attunement where real learning can take place. This is not the one-way mirror of interpretation characterized by psychoanalysis of old. Developmentally many of our patients have never experienced this type of an atmosphere as means of working through their emotional struggles. In such a therapeutic relationship a patient can recognize their problematic unconscious patterns and find more adaptive means of living and relieving their psychological distress. Richard Lane, a psychiatrist and researcher of psychotherapeutic change, captures a similar idea, he calls it the *corrective relational experience*. There is a natural convergence with Hall's lifetime of work and that captured in contemporary psychotherapeutic research. In other words, I think Hall is on the money...

References

Lane, R. D. (Ed.). (2020). *Neuroscience of enduring change: Implications for psychotherapy.* Oxford University Press.

Solms, M. (2021). *The hidden spring: a journey to the source of consciousness.* First edition. New York, W.W. Norton & Company.

Riffs on "The Power of Connection"

Lance Dodes

Jane Hall's book stands firmly in the tradition of investigation into the therapeutic nature of the relationship between patient and analyst. Her particular focus follows Freud's dictum, "Psychoanalysis is in essence a cure through love," a poetic summary of what is, indeed, one of the two main pillars of psychoanalysis. The other pillar could be stated as, "Psychoanalysis is in essence a cure through insight". At various times in the history of our field, and with various patients, one or the other of these central aspects has predominated. I will return to insight later.

Current advances in psychoanalysis

For the past 25 years or so, analytic technique and the definition of psychoanalysis itself have moved strongly away from restrictive, and hallowed, rules for conducting a proper analysis. Jane applauds the progress that has come with viewing psychoanalytic treatment as a co-creation in a 2-person psychology, with greater flexibility in the analyst, greater flexibility in the frequency of sessions and the use of furniture, and the use of remote treatment. Happily, she has embraced these changes without falling into the trap that has caught some others in their exuberance for the new freedoms and has not lost the essential values of neutrality (staying "neutral to the patient's conflict" (Hoffer)) and abstinence (refraining from enactments which arise from unconsidered emotional response to a patient's affects or actions). Jane's description of the importance of connection likewise avoids the potential problem of excessive self-disclosure or imposition of one's personal views on the patient. The equality that Jane recommends as an attitude between patient and analyst, therefore, includes the necessary guard rails that have always been understood to be part of psychoanalytic therapy.

An example of the equality Jane advises is to replace the word "interpretation" with "explanation." She sees "interpretation" as too authoritarian and less collaborative. Of course, one can offer an interpretation without being authoritarian. But I think Jane's point is not just about how the patient hears an interpretive comment, but about the attitude of the analyst offering it. She is urging us as therapists to be mindful of subtle ways we may unhelpfully influence the connection we build with patients.

It's been 80 years since Franz Alexander described the role of a corrective emotional experience in psychoanalysis (and he does not receive the credit he deserves for this, in my opinion). Hence, when Jane asks of her viewpoint about the central importance of emotional connection, "Dare I call this psychoanalysis?" there is no difficulty seeing how easily her views fit with long-held concepts of psychoanalysis, and agreeing when she answers her own question, "Yes".

Following Jane's lead in describing her book as "essays and riffs," what follows are riffs (associations?) on aspects of what she's written.

Riff 1. Insight

"Connection," the subject of this book, is described as "heart to heart communication … [which] often takes place without words." The other foundation of psychoanalytic therapy is quite different. It involves conscious, intellectual awareness by the patient of how their mind works (conflicts, unmet needs, usual defenses, etc.), and conscious awareness and understanding of the transference which has arisen from within them as a major part of the treatment. The benefits from this insight overlap with the benefits from less conscious aspects of the connection between patient and analyst, but insight is a separate, major goal of psychoanalytic treatment.

For example, in the case of Lisa, Jane writes, "Our relationship was very complicated, and I find the usual transference-countertransference thinking helpful but somehow inadequate. What seems to resonate more is the idea of me as container, and as a new object doling out food very slowly while holding a kicking, screaming infant who was also loving and lovable." This description is both accurate and elegant. However, I would not say it is separate or different from transference-countertransference. Lisa's kicking and screaming directed toward her analyst was an enactment of her transference in which Jane became her withholding and poisonous mother. The fact that Jane successfully functioned as a container in this situation can be described using transferential terms as an essential shared enactment of this transferential need. Alternatively, in another classic language, Jane serving in the role of container could be described as the required role-responsiveness to the role needed by the patient (Sandler). Regardless of the language we chose to describe the treatment, we would hope that Lisa left treatment with both aspects of successful psychoanalysis: the experience of being held, and conscious awareness of the transferential way she created this relationship in her analysis. The latter would mean she learned how and why she creates these deepest relationships. This insight would stand her in good stead for the rest of her life. Fortunately, Jane notes that "at the end of our work, Lisa grew to enjoy her new maturity. She learned about her omnipotent fantasy." That is, she had a corrective experience made possible by a deeply meaningful connection with her analyst, and she gained deeply important knowledge of herself which will strengthen her for the inevitable risks of repetition of her old feelings and behavior in the future. Either psychoanalytic result alone would be helpful, but incomplete.

Riff 2. Analytic versus non-analytic treatment

Appreciation of the role of insight in psychoanalysis, in addition to the corrective experience of meaningful connection, helps to avoid the mistaken notion that the nature and efficacy of psychoanalysis is explicable as just another version of the "common factors" in psychotherapy, such as empathy and formation of an alliance. One could, after all, point to a meaningful, even loving, connection between patient and therapist in non-analytic therapies. What distinguishes psychoanalytic treatment is both the specific depth of connection in analysis around the patient's central, generally unconscious issues, as Jane describes in Lisa's case, plus the depth of insight, usually achieved through understanding and working through the transference. Psychoanalysis may be a "cure through love" but it has to be a lot more than that to be psychoanalysis.

Riff 3. Language and Fads

Jane writes, "I also wonder how Lacanians, or Kohutians, or Bionians would have worked with Lisa." The mention of multiple languages brings up what I believe is a problem in our field: the repeated creation of new languages to describe similar concepts. New terminology can be a genuine advance in our perspective. But the wavelike nature of successive languages and concepts, with transient high cathexis of each new description, has the quality of a series of fads, each tending to fade with the next new thing, either because it is incorporated into previous knowledge or falls out of favor. One of many early examples included seeing a primal scene in a variety of clinical issues and dreams. The most important example has been Freud's Oedipus complex, which for a long time was (and for some people still is) central to psychoanalysis and psychoanalytic treatment. The enormous changes and advances in our knowledge of human psychology since Freud's time make it clear that seeing Oedipus as central to development, and therefore central to understanding the emotional problems of people, was the result of incomplete knowledge of human psychology in Freud's time. With our far greater breadth of understanding it's easy to see Oedipus as one stage of development whose significance, even when it is clinically relevant, is the result, not the cause, of the underlying issues facing the individual. Kohut's description of the failed first analysis of Mr. Z, which was predicated on the central nature of Oedipus, should have marked the end of the major importance for Oedipus. Here is what Kohut wrote of that first analysis:

"We had reached the oedipal conflict... It all seemed right, especially in view of the fact that it was accompanied by what appeared to be the unquestionable evidence of improvement... What was wrong at that time is much harder to describe than what seemed to be right. ...to state it bluntly, [it was] that the whole terminal phase... was... emotionally shallow... [It was only during the second analysis that] an underlying chronic despair [could be seen]" (Kohut).

Another example is Attachment theory. Once limited to early infant study it became applied to adults and all manner of cases. Attachment issues are real, of course. But for a time, Attachment became a widely used buzzword before fading to a more appropriate level as one of many ways to think about a person's psychological issues. Lisa's case is again an instance. Her longing for nurturance that was insufficiently supplied could probably be described in terms of disordered attachment. But that would be no better than using Kohutian concepts of inadequate mirroring and failure as a self-object. Or we could speak of the analyst's position in Lisa's case as a transitional object, a maternal object, or use Jane's language of a nurturing container.

Similarly, Jane mentions at another point that she finds it better to think of the term "dissociation" rather than another language/concept. "Dissociation" may be discussed in terms of vertical splitting, disavowal, repression, etc. It is another term that has enjoyed transient glory as a key concept which could be applied to a too-wide variety of clinical situations, but which now appears to have folded into existing theory as a useful variant without supplanting other explanatory language.

My point is that our field can do a better job acknowledging the overlap among favored theoretical terminologies, lest we elevate one language, and sometimes its developer, in a way that pushes psychoanalysis to be more like a group of belief systems than a science.

4. Neurobiology

Jane writes, "I imagined that the tension caused by a sibling's death and the worry that it could happen to her or to Tina was too much for her developing brain to handle." In my view, it would have been both sufficient and more correct to say her tension was "too much for her developing *mind* to handle," rather than her brain. It is speculation to include her brain here. Similarly, when Lisa is described as being delighted with her ability to redecorate her living room, Jane writes, "A lifting of depression might explain this, but I like to think that her brain rediscovered or even developed new abilities." In both these instances, brain function is introduced even though there is no necessity or evidence for it. I believe this is worth noticing because there has been pressure for some time to add a reference to the brain in our discussions, presumably in order to be considered up to date, or even to be considered more "scientific". Naturally, we are all interested in learning as much as possible about biological factors that influence our patients. But Complexity Theory taught us many years ago that no matter how much we learn about the workings of neurons or even their combined net-like connections, they cannot predict or explain the next, higher level of complexity we call Psychology. (The concept of Complexity, a part of modern physics, may be unfamiliar, but is illustrated by saying that we are all composed of molecules, yet no matter how complete is our knowledge of molecules, we cannot predict or explain life from that knowledge. Likewise, no matter how much we know about the structure of atomic nuclei we cannot, from that knowledge, predict or understand the operation of complex molecules. Every increase in complexity produces brand new properties that are neither present in, nor predictable from, the less complex level.

These new realities in more complex systems are appropriately called "emergent" properties or phenomena. Each science, therefore, takes you only so far. To understand the new properties and principles of the higher, more complex, system between molecules beyond the properties of its underlying atoms, you need a new science beyond Physics: Chemistry. Human psychology is an emergent phenomenon that occurs when billions of cells in the brain create a complex system. It has new properties that can only be understood through a new science: Psychology. [Waldrup]).

Psychoanalysis has suffered forever with trying to explain itself in terms acceptable to non-analysts, particularly other physicians. This has led to either defensive ignoring other fields or the reverse, an effort to appear more scientific by incorporating their language. In Lisa's case, Jane has given us a clear understanding of her psychology. To introduce a speculative non-psychological explanation is not only unnecessary, but it also devalues the truth and value of what she says.

Conclusion

Jane Hall has written a valuable book about the current state of psychoanalysis, emphasizing a plea to focus on its essential humanity. Her description of the therapeutic value of the relationship between analyst and patient as a deeply meaningful, developmentally important connection, rings as true today as it has ever been.

In riffing on her comments, I've underlined the importance of insight as a separate, core element of psychoanalysis, which together with the connection about which Jane writes, makes psychoanalysis what it is.

I've also argued that our field has suffered with devotion to particular favored terms and concepts, overlooking how much these languages, valuable though they may be, mainly overlap with each other. At the same time, I noted that there has been persistent devotion to, and overuse of, ideas which are no longer central to modern thinking, to the detriment of individual understanding of patients. I offered Freud's Oedipus complex as an example, using Kohut's account of the two analyses of Mr. Z as illustration.

Finally, I suggested that insertion into discussion of individual cases of neurobiological ideas that have neither evidence nor relevance, obscures and degrades the value of the psychological knowledge we do legitimately possess. It also ignores the lessons of Complexity theory which tell us that human psychology cannot be reduced to or explained by knowledge of the less complex system from which it has emerged, because like all such emergent systems, it has properties that are not present in the underlying structure from which it has emerged.

References

Hoffer, Axel (1985). Toward a Definition of Psychoanalytic Neutrality. *JAPA* 33:771–795.

Kohut, H. (1979) The Two Analyses of Mr. Z. *International Journal of Psychoanalysis* 60:3–27.

Sandler, J. (1976). Countertransference and role-responsiveness. *International Review of Psycho-Analysis,* 3(1):43–47.

Waldrop M. (1992). *Complexity: the emerging science at the edge of order and chaos.* New York: Touchstone Books.

Riffing on a Riff
On Jane Hall's Riff on Listening

David Lichtenstein

The origins of *riff* as a musical concept in jazz are hard to place. It has been widely used by jazz musicians since the 1920s and is indispensable in talking and writing about jazz. Of the different explanations of its origin, the one that seems most plausible to me is that it is a playful abbreviation of *refrain*, a common musical term based on the Old French word *refraindre*, which simply means *to repeat*. A musical refrain or riff is a repeated musical element, figure, or theme. As a musical phrase that the song returns to and repeats, it challenges the player to play. Consider the common expression 'that old refrain' for an idea that has been repeated too many times without innovation or nuance. There is always the danger of repetition that it becomes repetitive.

A riff as a repeated element in jazz, and by extension now in rock and R&B, can likewise become banal and repetitive. The challenge to the musician is always to bring life to the riff, to "make it new," as Ezra Pound wrote, quoting an ancient Chinese proverb about the challenge to the poet. Quoting the ancients in a new context, creating a new sense, is itself a riff.

To riff, as an action, is to do something precisely opposite to playing that same old refrain. Rather than playing a tired repetition, riffing creates playful variations on a theme in a way that generates new versions: making it new. To riff is never merely to play the riff but always to play with it.

As a noun, a riff means both the repeated element and the new variation on that repeated element. It switches meaning depending on its use. This switch is not incidental. Repetition provokes the relation between sameness and difference, the dialectic of the new, as Kierkegaard showed in his essay On Repetition (1843).

The riff is the dialectic of the new. It is about play and signification, about the interplay of repetition and innovation. It is essential not only to art but to speaking and listening as well. This dialectic is the key to Jane Hall's discussion about Jazz and Psychoanalysis and the relationship between them.

It is not incidental to this discussion that Freud considered the compulsion to repeat to be a fundamental expression of the Death Drive. He then went on to say that this drive was never found on its own but always intertwined with the Erotic Drive to create and to play. The intertwining of repetition and innovation is at the heart of psychoanalytic theory and the practice of psychoanalysis, as any analysand knows well from experience.

Riffing on a theme is an essential part of jazz. I suspect that jazz musicians coined the term riff because one of the things that distinguishes what they do is to repeat the refrain by playing with it, to improvise variations on the theme, to repeat a musical idea or phrase in a new way, however paradoxical that may be. How a repetition can be new and still a repetition is at the heart of jazz improvisation. And although improvisation is not unique to jazz, there was a great deal of improvisation in European classical music and certainly in African and Asian musical traditions, it is at the heart of jazz in a way that is new in the history of music and essential to the idiom.

The word riff itself is autological. It is an instance of what it means. That is, it is itself a playful riff on the word refrain and on the conceptual interplay of repetition and innovation. As a signifier formed by its own meaning, it demonstrates that we riff in language just as we riff in music. Jazz musicians often riffed in their speech to the point where this became as much a part of the jazz scene as the improvisatory character of the music. The frequent use of neologism, onomatopoeia, and autology, such as *be-bop, Scat, or Jam,* suggests that Jazz is also a mode of expression beyond music. Jazz culture is a celebration of improvisation and a playful relation to language, not simply a school of music that employs improvisation. Indeed, the term jazz itself, apart from the music, has a range of meanings around play, vigor, vitality, and sex.

That there is a relationship between play and sex is another truth shared by jazz and psychoanalysis. It is not just sex play but the challenge and pleasure in finding something new in the repetition of the physical act that is essential to how the 'talking cure' works. Sex and love might be an old refrain unless riffing brings them back to life. Indeed, that riffing with one's analyst can bring life to one's loving is certainly at the heart of Freud's great discovery.

What is essential in psychoanalysis is to be found in the act of saying, in its playful and risky improvisation in the face of repetition, more than in the resulting text of what is said. In other words, the discursive act is the key to the psychoanalytic process more than the accumulated knowledge of self that results from the saying. The change that comes about in psychoanalysis is less about knowing more than it is about a different kind of knowing, one that comes into being through the act of speaking, indeed through riffing on memories and events, and especially on the moment of speaking and being heard in itself. If it works, psychoanalysis jazzes our experience of being as a being with and for the other.

Being heard suggests that the other is listening and that is not self-evident. In the fullest sense listening is as sensitive to the process of play and repetition that I am discussing here as is speaking. This is where Jane Hall's essay really takes off. It is not simply a riff on jazz and psychoanalysis, but a riff on listening and its functions in jazz and psychoanalysis, indeed its functions precisely in relation to the play of improvisation. How to hear the play, the riffing that is going on, is a sort of counterplay. Hall's title, Riff on Listening, suggests that in the counterplay that is listening, there is a kind of riffing as well. Freud called this 'evenly suspended attention,' but that overly technical phrase only begins to capture the complex activity of psychoanalytic listening. I would suggest that the key to psychoanalytic listening is hearing the play in speaking that the speaker is not necessarily aware of, caught up as s(he) is in the speech act itself. It is hearing the riffs, in both senses, the repeated themes, and the play on those themes in the analytic discourse.

Hall's Riff on Listening is not only a playful examination of the art of listening in jazz and psychoanalysis but also an invitation to a series of listening experiences. She provides a wonderfully curated series of links that show what she is saying. It is only in the act of listening that meaning can be encountered. Hall makes the fundamental point that a psychoanalyst, first and foremost, needs to know how to listen but to listen in a distinctive way that is more akin to being another player in a musical ensemble than to being a rational agent seeking to clarify symptoms, lapses, and inhibitions as a removed observer.

This is an innovative and somewhat controversial view of the analyst's function. It suggests an interplay on the level of the discourse that makes the analyst's function as that of one who hears and supports the play in discourse. Hall's essay is called a Riff on Listening, but it could be a Riff on Hearing. It is possible to listen and not hear. To know how to listen is to understand what is to hear.

Hall opens her essay with a quote from Duke Ellington, viz. "The most important thing I look for in a musician is whether he knows how to listen." What does it mean to 'know-how to listen'? Surely, this is about keeping your ears open to the play of the sounds and their meaning effects. A Riff on Listening is about listening to the riff.

She concludes her essay with the following statement about psychoanalysis:

In sum, if we listen to and play with each other over time, we hear all kinds of utterances, moods, styles, contradictions, emotions, rigidities that shift, all making prediction dangerous. It is the surprises in analytic work and in music that have kept me going—and I wish the same for you.

Hall offers several links to what she tells is her favorite song, *All the Things You Are* (Kern/ Hammerstein, 1939), as perhaps the central illustration of her ideas. She also provides links to two discussions of the song's structure, one by the great guitarist Jim Hall, who was Jane's husband. This personal dimension of the essay adds another layer of significance to the discussion. This is not an academic essay but a deeply personal one about both music and psychoanalysis.

As Hall's essay shows us, a riff is not merely a demonstration of technical skill or theoretical sophistication but a deeply personal engagement with the Other, whether as the voice in the music or the unknown resonances in the analysand's speech.

Homo sum, humani nihil a me alienum puto
On "Story telling"

Luba Kessler

Having told throughout her book the story of how she connects with her patients, Jane Hall arrives at its penultimate chapter to consider the psychoanalytic role of storytelling itself. Here the many clinical vignettes and insights in the book find a home in the appreciation of the stories by patients and dedicated healers alike.

Her endeavor proceeds from a place of open-minded generosity of interest. She credits Ella Sharpe with the instruction for "deep seated curiosity" as the most indispensable working principle. There are no "real true" stories. "Happy stories" are dangerous. Hall is guided by the deep understanding that the spoken, and as yet unspoken, latent stories contain trauma, fantasy, rage, love, your name it—in fact, the naming articulation of their existence is what allows their therapeutic reformation. What accompanies the work along the way is "common sense" and tactful trust in the capacity for connection, even when silence precludes speech and so requires patience and nonverbal attunement. This is, in various permutations, what Jane Hall's consummate account is about.

Genuine humanist interest and intent permeate her work, guided by psychoanalytically informed listening. It is possible to see how it liberates her spontaneity, and how that in turn frees the patient to respond in kind, enhancing therapeutic connectedness. This spontaneity derives from clinical astuteness and a comfortable use of therapeutic technique. But it is also amplified by an openness to being informed by other fields as well. Hall's learning curiosity brings her to consider neuroscientific insights in the interest of applying them to her psychoanalytic acumen. Immersive appreciation of music, literature, art serve to amplify the emotional resonance she curates in the work with her patients. Hall draws from every source that enhances it. She is grateful to psychoanalytic fellow travelers who, like her, found storytelling an inspired way to think about patients and their work with each of them; or others who advocated tuning in to seemingly incomprehensibly disordered stories told by psychotic patients.

The initial reaction to the chapter on storytelling is likely to be one of as if reading a self-evident testimonial. Mine was, and caused doubt about offering a commentary: what could possibly be added? Every therapist hears patients' stories, starting with the 'cases' in their clinical training, including Freud's famous case histories at the foundation of psychoanalysis. Yet, further reflection on this seemingly self-evidentiary nature invited a question: What is it that gives the storytelling its incontrovertibly compelling power? As far back as in the Old Testament the therapeutics of 19/20th century psychoanalysis are foretold in the Book of Job by a character who says, "I will speak that I may find relief" (Job 32:20, in Soloveitchik, 2018). What makes stories indispensable?

It becomes illuminating, as well as simultaneously humbling yet affirming then to see that psychoanalytic listening to stories represents an amazing development in the biological evolution of life, with the humanistic expansion of mentation as its apogee to date (It is yet to be seen what transformations will come about in the aftermath of the algorithmic manufacture of storytelling by human-engendered artificial intelligence.) Individual storytelling is a product of millennial development of the human race while individual stories are an ontogenetic achievement for every person.

In his 2024 book *The Language Puzzle: Piecing Together The Six-Million-Year Story of How Words Evolved* an archeologist Steven Mithen looks at findings from the fields of archeology, anthropology, linguistics, psychology, genetics, ethnology, anatomy and neuroscience. It provides an interesting interdisciplinary exposition of evolutionary intersections between biology and cultural transmission. Over many millennia, language develops as a system of communication in human society, and in turn influences human perception and thought. It makes it possible to convey stories of experience, develop abstract and metaphoric meanings out of them, enhance communal adaptations by their sharing, and create culture. It is this broad evolutionary and cultural human inheritance that met its application in the psychological study and treatment of patients at the end of the 19th century, and it continues to ground and animate the finely attuned work of psychoanalysts such as Jane Hall's. Is it any wonder then that she draws her inspiration for and her prowess in it from all: patients, teachers, students, art, music, literature? Constrained by the commonality of shared anatomical and cognitive Homo Sapiens features, humans nevertheless have developed variations in both to account for great linguistic diversity. That diversity finds its most exquisite expression yet in the uniqueness of every being and every life. Informed by the outlines and formulations of her clinical and theoretical knowledge of psychology, the analyst is ready to hear every patient in their singular embeddedness in the personal, familial and social storylines. Thus, does she prepare for the intricate work of tending to human wellbeing.

Patients respond to Hall's open minded therapeutic curiosity in listening to their stories because of the manifest empathy of her reception of them. It made me think that her lifelong listening immersion in music, and perhaps especially in the creative improvisational flexibility of jazz, promoted a particular fluidity of mind. She could adjust the 'keys' and the 'vibes' to tune in, allowing for the *einfuhlung,* the *feeling with another,* that makes possible the establishment of therapeutic trust. But it is not empathy for its own sake alone that seems to be at work for Hall. There is respect and pleasure in the individuality of each patient, which gives each of them, and the story each brings to tell, a compelling reason to matter, and thus be worthy of being told and heard. What makes it possible to conjoin them to deploy the empathetic interest in individuality? Psychoanalytic theorizing by various schools of thought, aided by infant/child research and neuroscientific findings have provided rich insights into their development by examining the psychic conditions of early life. Hall's clinical and theoretical acumen is deeply informed by her interest and integrated knowledge of them.

It turns out, though, that before the advent of psychoanalysis, or psychology as such in general, an interesting attempt at elucidating the processes responsible for both intersubjectivity of empathy and individuality took place in the Age of Enlightenment by philosopher Jean Jacques Rousseau. He advanced the thought that the process of forming the idea of an "I" develops as the *individual identifies with* those he perceives as like himself, earning the credit of being a pivotal theorist of the formation of the individual selfhood through intersubjectivity and mutual recognition. To him, the formation of a distinct "self" and self-consciousness, or personal identity is part of a developmental process, one that is the result of a process of the individual interacting with the environment and especially with one's fellow human beings. And, in the spirit of the age, he extends the concepts of identity and identification not only to individual development but also to the development of human society (Scott, 2024).

It is likely not a coincidence that Rousseau's innovative and influential thought in this regard dovetailed with the establishment of the scientific field of ethnology in the 18th century. After nearly three centuries of sea travel to distant lands encountering foreign ethnicities and societies, it may have been the new field of ethnology that in its interest in other cultures was guided by a social sense of mutuality, paving the way for the evolution of intersubjectivity of empathy. Encountering 'others' made it possible to awaken to it and to observe it. And so, Rousseau found affectionate recognition for his intuition of empathic identification in the 1962 speech *Jean-Jacque Rousseau, Founder of the Sciences of Man* by the 20th century ethnologist Claude Levy-Strauss (Levy-Strauss, 1976).

When an analyst speaks of storytelling by her patient, as Hall does in her chapter and throughout her book. she in effect reports on traversing a boundary and visiting an 'other'. Her manner of recounting an individual history along with its particular personal mythology is not altogether dissimilar to that of an ethnologist. Not entirely unlike him in relation to the inhabitant tribe of a foreign land, she tunes in to the abstract poetry of shareable metaphor so as to be able to decipher their individual psychological significance in her patient's case while at the same time learning the specific lexicon of the patient's way of transmitting intrinsic personal meanings. What drives each of them on in those pursuits? What is the motivation for such curiosity in the other tribe/person and what might be the consequence?

Rousseau offers strikingly modern formulations that pertain (Scott, 2024), which may impress an analyst for their resonance with Freud's formulations a century and a half later:

> "The positive or attracting action is the simple work of nature, which seeks to extend and reinforce the sentiment of our being; the negative or repelling action, which compresses and diminishes the being of another, is a combination produced by reflection. From the former arise all the loving and gentle passions, and from the latter all the hateful and cruel passions."

"There is a purely passive physical and organic sensitivity [sensibilité] which seems to have as its end only the preservation of our bodies and of our species through the direction of pleasure and pain."

"when the strength of an expansive soul has me identify myself [m'identifie] with my fellow, and I feel that I am, so to speak, in him, it is in order not to suffer that I do not want him to suffer. I am interested in him for love of myself"

When an ethnologist travels to a distant land s/he expands and alters her being and that of her own society by entering—and identifying with—another culture. The analyst does something similar when entering the story of her patient's experience. She, too, will not be the same in consequence of those encounters. Hall knows this when she expresses her gratitude to her patients, her colleagues and students: they expand the sphere of her own understanding and wisdom, readying it for transmission to others patients, students and readers of her book.

Are there any possible pitfalls to be aware of? Surely—if the analogy to ethnology holds— this is not an altogether idle question. The attractions of visiting distant lands brought with them expansions in the form of exploitation and colonization. Is there a cautionary note in this for psychoanalysis and psychoanalyst?

Here's Rousseau again:

"Pity is sweet because, in putting ourselves in the place of the one who suffers, we nevertheless feel the pleasure of not suffering as he does" (Emile, 219–21).

An analyst might frown at, or smile in recognition of, this suggestion and perhaps the gentle rebuke it represents. Is this a latent, i. e. hidden, motive of the work we otherwise consider laudable for its healing purposes? And if that is so, is it a necessary, if also unavoidable, aspect of it? An analyst needs to know, but not succumb to, the pain of suffering. This is her responsibility: to know the pain so that she could be of help to the suffering of others.

When at the end of the 19th century, Freud veered from the strictly neuroscientific pursuits to founding psychoanalysis on the strength of the stories in the Studies on Hysteria, he brought the enlightenment of the preceding ages into the psychological project of improving human lot. To do that, he devised a new language to teach about 'transference' and 'countertransference' so as to forge the path to empathic communion with an other, including the other within the analyst herself. It is this nesting dolls mutuality that Jane Hall's spotlight on storytelling helps us to bear in mind.

References

Levy-Strauss, C. (1976). *Structural Anthropology*. Vol. II. Basic Books, Inc., New York.

Mithen, S. (2024). *The Language Puzzle: Piecing Together the Six-Million-Year Story of How Words Evolved*. Basic Books, New York.

Scott, J. T. (2024). Rousseau and the Development of Identity. *Political Research Quarterly,* 77(1), 359–370. https://doi.org/10.1177/10659129231212901

Soloveitchik, J. (2018) *The Lonely Man of Faith*. OU Press. Maggid Books, Jerusalem.

Musings on Jane Hall's Conversation with Martin S. Bergmann

Daniel Benveniste

I had heard that Martin Bergmann (1913–2014) was a distinguished analyst, so as he walked down the center aisle of the conference hall in Berlin in 2007 and we silently passed each other, I thought to myself, *"I wish I could have known him."* But I never did, and that is why Jane Hall's 1988 and 2008 interviews with him, published together in her book *The Power of Connection* (2022), was of special interest to me.

Jane's interview is casual yet informative, and it beautifully preserves the affection between a student and teacher. It's a lovely interview and has aspects that remind me of my clinical mentor, Nathan Adler (1911–1994). After reading Jane's interview, I found and read Fredric T. Perlman's outstanding article "Love and Its Objects: On the Contributions to Psychoanalysis of Martin S. Bergmann" (*Psychoanalytic Review*, Vol. 86, No. 6, 1999). In it I discovered that Bergmann's father, Hugo Bergmann, was a philosopher and friend of Martin Buber and that Hugo Bergmann's son, Martin Bergmann (yes, named after Martin Buber), had been intrigued in his youth by a small book written by

Siegfried Bernfeld (1892–1953) "on the application of psychoanalytic principles to the problem of educating children orphaned by war." What is not stated in the Perlman article is that Bernfeld was Buber's assistant, later a psychoanalyst and close associate of Sigmund Freud in Vienna. After moving to San Francisco in 1937 Bernfeld became Nathan Adler's mentor—my mentor's mentor. As I read Jane Hall's interview of Martin Bergmann, I felt the teaching styles and psychoanalytic attitudes of Siegfried Bernfeld and Nathan Adler resonating in the background. Bernfeld, Bergmann, and Adler were all well known for their ability to speak about psychoanalysis eloquently and without notes. Of course, Freud had the same gift.

As an interesting aside, Arnold D. Richards, also a friend of Martin Bergmann, told me that Hugo Bergmann, the philosopher, and Gershom Sholom, the famous scholar of Jewish mysticism, were friends and that at some point along the way they both divorced their wives, and each married the wife of the other. This, as Richards explained, angered Martin Bergmann and led to a special interest in the role of the mother in psychological development and the consequences of maternal loss.

Early in Jane's interview, Bergmann says, "I think the young analyst of today, whether they like it or not, is confronted with a multiplicity of models. If he decided to join a particular organization, he can be sure that he will be subjected, perhaps mercilessly, to the one model and would be discouraged from interest in the other models. I would urge the opposite" (all quotes from Hall and Bergmann are from her interview with him in *The Power of Connection*). His advice is for the student to learn as much as one can about the model one is first introduced to, "but afterwards explore the other models available. Because you'll always learn something from them. That is, I don't regard any deviant school as having nothing to contribute." I like Bergmann's ecumenical approach to theory and have practiced it in my own professional development.

I think of models of the mind as "lenses," as ways of looking at the psyche and the clinical situation. Each lens brings some things into high relief and recesses other things into low relief. The medical model highlights tissue damage, injuries, hormones, genetics, neurological structure, and biochemistry. The cognitive behavioral model highlights stimuli, responses, reinforced behaviors, cognitive maps, learning, and beliefs. The family systems model highlights family structure, roles, alliances, and communication patterns. The psychoanalytic model highlights unconscious motivations, defenses, object relations, resistances, transferences, and the repetition compulsion. And when Bergmann speaks of the analysts today being confronted by a multiplicity of models, he is, of course, speaking of the multiple models within the context of broader psychoanalytic theory, including ego psychology, object relations theory, self-psychology, modern conflict theory, the French school, and relational psychology. Accepting any one of them as a personal religion with its corresponding saints and mythologies is common practice, but it is a grave error. And, of course, when one accepts one theory as a religion along with it comes a stance against the enemy camps. It is a very common and highly unprofessional stance. Clinical thinking is critical thinking about clinical matters. From that perspective we need to ask what explanatory power or utility each theory offers us in our work with our patients.

Bergmann says, "Many students today no longer understand Freud. So that I have to reiterate it in a language which is a little closer to them. This is particularly true with certain difficult books like *The Ego and the Id*. One has to read it almost line by line because the book is no longer accessible. So, the teacher has a fundamentally different task, and that is to act as a bridge between the students and what Freud said." I found this refreshing to read. There are so many Freud bashers and detractors today that young students learn from their teachers that Freud was wrong and is passe before they ever even read his works. Bergmann describes himself as "a bridge between the students and what Freud said." I think this is also the role some of the modern psychoanalytic writers serve today. They can talk about Freud and psychoanalysis in a modern language and a modern style that young people can better understand. Personally, I have always been fascinated and inspired by Freud's writings, but one of the most important bridge functions that I serve for my students is to emphasize how important it is to read Freud through a metaphoric lens. Most objections to psychoanalytic theory are literal interpretations of psychoanalytic concepts.

Jane Hall notes that psychoanalytic training is typically organized around analysis, supervision, and seminars; she also points out that Bergmann is well known for his seminars that took place every Friday of the week for decades. People often debate which of the three pillars is more important. I think the answer is very personal and may even change during one's life, but I have no doubt that Bergmann was an exceptional seminar leader and probably inspired curiosity in addition to teaching content.

In the interview, Bergmann also says, "Freud was interested in creating a science. A science is based on repetitive phenomena. Science does not prepare us for the unique and special, at least not in an obvious way. So that, to some extent, Freud's eagerness to have psychoanalysis recognized as a science tended to work against the recognition of the uniqueness of the analyst and the uniqueness of the patient." This consideration gives us pause when evaluating psychoanalytic psychotherapy outcome studies, formalized psychoanalytic training, and the vicissitudes of supervision.

As a Ph.D. psychologist, Martin Bergmann didn't have the option of receiving his training at a standard American Psychoanalytic Association institute (which only accepted MD candidates at the time); instead, he sought unofficial training by entering analysis with Edith Jacobson and attending seminars led by Paul Federn, Theodor Reik, and Robert Waelder. Bergmann operated independently until 1952, when he was invited to teach at Reik's National

Psychological Association for Psychoanalysis. Other opportunities for teaching within the American Psychoanalytic Association became possible for Bergmann after the 1988 lawsuit that opened up psychoanalytic training for non-M.D. analysts.

Siegfried Bernfeld, whom I mentioned earlier, was himself a psychologist and similarly made unauthorized analytic training available to Nathan Adler and a few others in San Francisco in the late 1930s, '40s, and '50s. Adler was also a psychologist and not permitted formal institute training. I recall sitting next to Nathan in a meeting in which the implications of the 1988 lawsuit were being discussed. In the discussion, he stood up and delivered a mea culpa for not having launched the suit himself decades ago. He returned to his seat, next to me, and whispered, "Well, we know how the psychiatrists have ruined psychoanalysis; now we're going to find out how the psychologists will ruin it!"

Martin Bergmann's educational style is illuminated in Jane's interview, and it reminded me of the open and creative teaching style that Bernfeld described in his famous paper "On Psychoanalytic Training" (1962). It is a well-thought-out challenge to some of the consequences of institute training that he had encountered in Vienna, Berlin, and San Francisco. Bernfeld was an inspired teacher, an eloquent lecturer, and a passionate idealist who remained committed to the primary prerogatives of students and their freedom to grow despite the encroachments of bureaucratic institutions. He abhorred authoritarian administration-centered institutions that stifled students and their creativity. He had flourished in the Vienna and Berlin institutes primarily because they were new, unstructured, and he was free to teach as he saw fit. With the establishment of the American institutes, psychoanalysis and psychoanalytic training became formalized, and Bernfeld experienced these institutions as a constriction of the psychoanalytic ethos. In "On Psychoanalytic Training," posthumously published in 1962, he presented a vision of another kind of a psychoanalytic institute. He described an institute that would be student-centered and progressive in its teaching approach. There would be few formal requirements for admission other than a passionate interest and talent for psychoanalysis. Study would take place in small groups and attention would largely be on the interests of the individual students. The focus would not be on formal admission requirements or the fulfillment of prescribed educational tasks but on the interests and talents of each individual student, their relationship with the teacher, and the pursuit of their creative psychoanalytic work.

Based on Jane Hall's interview with Martin Bergmann, I could not help but recognize a style similar to what Siegfried Bernfeld had described and the manner in which he conducted the unofficial seminar that Nathan Adler had attended. Bergmann's studies with Federn, Reik, and Waelder certainly would have been informed by the same Viennese psychoanalytic spirit that Bernfeld had been immersed in.

Jane Hall asks Bergmann, "If you were a student today, just starting out, where would you find the best education in psychoanalysis? Would you find it in the institute, or would you find it in private seminars where the students could select different teachers for long periods of time?" And Bergmann replies, "I would hate to answer that question."

What makes Jane's question so difficult to answer? I think the answer is that psychoanalytic training throws one into the unconscious dynamics of the group. These dynamics have indeed helped a few people to develop their psychoanalytic skills and build a career. But many coming out of North American traditions of the 20th century were infantilized or stunted in the process and others were frankly crushed by the experience.

What follows here may sound like a non sequitur but stay with me as it is a direct continuation of this theme of creative or oppressive psychoanalytic education. I have long been fascinated by the Oedipus complex, and my only critique is that it is often regarded too literally and not metaphorically enough. Aside from that, regarding the relationship between the Oedipus complex and American psychoanalytic organizations in the 20th century, I have observed that American psychoanalysis was significantly influenced by the same cultural trends that gave rise to the generation gap. It was the generation gap between the fathers, or the establishment, and their sons, or the next generation, in American psychoanalytic organizations.

Now, I am an outsider to American psychoanalytic organizational life, but as a psychoanalytically oriented clinical psychologist, a colleague of many analysts, and, more importantly, as a psychoanalytic historian, I have observed the tendency of the fathers, or the leaders of American psychoanalytic institutes, to raise the standards that in turn raised the age of admissions to institutes. They found reasons to exclude candidates, reasons to keep them in training for seven, eight, nine, ten years, and to demand that candidates conform to the theoretical and technical demands of the fathers. The desires, ambitions, and creativity of the candidates were often seen as resistances, manifestations of the Oedipus complex, and efforts to kill the father. Thus, the American psychoanalytic fathers (the establishment) did their best to hold the candidates down without recognizing that the only way for psychoanalysis to continue would be for the fathers to teach the candidates well and pass the torch of psychoanalysis to the next generation. This tendency of the fathers, the organization, to stifle creativity, snuff out ambition, exclude candidates, hold back advancement, and in other ways limit the next generation of psychoanalysts is what I call a manifestation of the "Laius complex in American psychoanalysis."

You may recall that Laius was Oedipus's father. But Laius had a history before Oedipus was even born. Laius was entrusted to teach a young boy, Chrysippus, how to drive a chariot, but instead of doing so, he raped the young boy. His punishment for this, as told to him by the Oracle, was that his firstborn son would kill him and marry his wife. So, when the time came and Laius's wife, Jocasta, gave birth, Laius decided to kill his own son by having his feet pinned and then taken out and left to die on a mountainside. Now, get this picture: Laius molested a young boy; tried but failed to have his infant son, Oedipus, killed on a mountainside; and years later when he met Oedipus on the road, he tried to kill him again! What a dad!

This, from my perspective, is what organized American psychoanalysis did in the second half of the 20th century. It was possessed by its Laius complex. It did its very best to hold down, exclude, and limit the creativity of the next generation, and by the 1980s they almost drove psychoanalysis into extinction. And you know something interesting? They didn't do that in Latin America—and I don't think they do that so much anymore in the United States either. But I think in the second half of the 20th century it was fairly common, and it stunted psychoanalysis.

Nonetheless, there have been rare teachers like Siegfried Bernfeld, Nathan Adler, Arnold D. Richards, and, apparently Martin Bergmann as well, who had what I would call a "Polybus complex." Polybus and Merope were the king and queen of Corinth, who adopted the infant Oedipus and kindly raised him to adulthood. Those with a Polybus complex are the teachers that run interference between Laius (the hostile teachers) and Oedipus (the students) in an effort to give psychoanalysis, and the next generation of psychoanalysts, a chance at a future.

Jane Hall asks, "What do you think people like about Bion? Bion seems to be so popular these days. There are study groups that are going on, Bionion, which I don't understand, but I feel I probably should know more about this." To which Bergmann replies, "Why should you?... What is it that you don't understand about your patients that you think Bion could help you with?" Bergmann also refers to the way psychoanalysis has a history of writers giving new names to old concepts and acting like they had discovered a new school of thought. This is what Nathan Adler used to describe as "putting old wine in new bottles."

In Jane Hall's interview, Bergmann makes several references to the importance of psychoanalytic history for the clinician. Bernfeld was also interested in psychoanalytic history and wrote some of the original articles on Freud's biography. Analysts who orient themselves to psychoanalytic history have a depth of understanding that transcends the latest fads in psychoanalysis. It enables them to recognize authentic extensions of psychoanalytic theory and differentiate them from the so-called innovations that are nothing more than old resistances to the radical and subversive nature of psychoanalysis.

I recall that when I began studying psychology in San Francisco, in 1972, it seemed that everyone was talking about Erik Erikson, Fritz Perls, and Carlos Castaneda. By 1975 there were posters on all the walls, even on telephone poles, advertising seminars and lectures on the work of C. G. Jung and Wilhelm Reich, which had become all the craze. By the mid-1980s it was all about Kohut, Kernberg, and Masterson. By the late 1980s everyone seemed to be talking about British object relations and Lacan. Then came the fascination with Bion, and then came those who sought to integrate, compare, and contrast Bion with Winnicott and the French analysts. Then came the pandemic and the "tyranny of the real"—the external reality dominated, the real relationship became the focus, and the real analyst and the real training became the top concern. The tyranny of the real immediately excluded unconscious motivation, the Oedipus complex, and transference. What's next? Nathan Adler used to quote John Dewey, "Democracy has to be borne anew every generation, and education is its midwife." He would then add that psychoanalysis has to be born anew in every generation as well. We should ask ourselves now, are we currently (2024) killing psychoanalysis or helping it to be born anew?

Jane also asks Bergmann about the tradition of exclusion in American psychoanalysis. He replies, "But when I wish to be included, and I am included, there is no guarantee that I won't say, 'Well, now that I'm included, it is time to exclude.' Because there is the wish to belong, but the wish also not to let anybody in."

Bergmann's reflections naturally remind me of the tendency of psychoanalytic societies to split in two, which W. Ernest Freud described as a process of mitosis. It also reminds me of the old Sephardic saying, "Two Jews, three temples."

Jane continues with the line of questioning about exclusion and the way that students, as a group, sometimes become annoyed with one student in the seminar. Bergmann replies, "That happens many times. The class combines against a particular member of the class and wants the teacher to do something about it."

"So, what happens then?" she asks. Bergmann replies, "You explain to the class that this is the phenomenon of aggression, and if you exclude this culprit, another culprit will appear. So, we might as well deal with this culprit.... I remember that I realized this in the army. Every company had to have a scapegoat. But who was chosen as the scapegoat was determined by certain psychological conditions."

Jane asks, "Masochism?" Bergmann replies, "Masochism, intelligence, not fighting back. There are certain things."

Reading this short list of characteristics that predispose one to exclusion, I began to reflect on the history of psychoanalysis, and it seems to me that some of the most famous exclusions of individuals from psychoanalytic organizations were people who were extremely creative, unique, perhaps a bit odd, and some with a voracious hunger for knowledge.

My musings on Jane's interview with Martin Bergmann are simply my own reflections on the themes raised in the interview. What is not captured in my musings is how

Bergmann was obviously such a brilliant analyst and also such a mensch—such a regular guy. Also not captured in my musings is the affection between Jane, the loving student, and Bergmann, the loving teacher. I finished reading their dialogue still wishing I had met Bergmann but feeling that through Jane Hall's beautiful interview I had, in a sense, met him. And for that I am very grateful.

References

Bernfeld, S. (1962). On psychoanalytic training. *Psychoanalytic Quarterly*, Vol. 31, Issue 4, pp. 453–482.

Hall, J. (2022). *The Power of Connection*. IPBooks.

Perlman, Fredric T. (1999). Love and its objects: On the contributions to psychoanalysis of Martin S. Bergmann. *Psychoanalytic Review*, Vol. 86, No. 6. pp. 915–963.

A Conversation with Jane Hall:
Therapist of Uniquity

M. Sagman Kayatekin

MSK: What I want to do in these sessions with you Jane is, maybe just as you suggest, focus on the book and then branch out from there. I have some questions but you're free to improvise. So that this is not fully structured. This conversation is about you and this work of yours and it can go in any direction it will take us. Is there anything you want to start with in the today's meeting

JH: Do you want to know who I am, a little bit about me?

MSK: I think you're well-known, but it would help the reader to give them some idea. I definitely want to know and as much as you think is pertinent.

JH: OK. well, I'm semi-retired so I have time to reflect. I still do supervision, consultation, and I teach but I stopped seeing patients about four years ago. Because, when I work with people I see them for long periods of time, and when I turned 80, I started thinking about how long I would be alert and around and so I stopped accepting new patients and started winding down. I ended with my last analytic case after a planned termination in July 2019 and with bitter-sweet feelings, closed my office door for the last time. I was looking forward to some travel, seeing old friends, and pursuing more knowledge, especially about the brain.

Also, I have been writing on and off over my professional career—actually since second grade when I wrote a mystery story in installments for the weekly class paper—and I had a few papers that I hadn't published over the years, so this book is a compilation of some of those papers. The idea of third book was a little scary because I had changed much of my thinking, but Arnie Richards really encouraged me.

I kind of critiqued the classical technique and theory I had learned. I graduated from a classical institute in 1981. It was very strict; I mean we weren't allowed to mention Melanie Klein so that's how strict it was. Bion, so popular today, was not even on our horizon. Winnicott yes! I always had four or five analytic cases that had started in psychotherapy and my colleagues (at NYFS) wanted to know how come. I knew I paid attention to what I had been taught but I had also studied and graduated from Ruben and Gertrude Blank's Institute, ISP, before and during my early NYFS years. So, I think the blending of these two approaches, one where the focus was on the "less structured" patients—the so-called borderline—and the other on the so-called neurotic level patients. Building the ego versus analysis of defense at first confused me but as I synthesized these approaches I became a good clinician. I think more patients than we realize need both at different moments in a treatment. I hadn't been aware of how I evolved but as I look back, I see the roots. We were taught to just interpret the patient's material—not to answer questions —and to be like a blank screen at CFS. I remember one teacher who told us that we shouldn't even have paintings on our wall in the office because that would tell too much about us. I'm sure none of us followed that advice but we were taught that patients would find it easier to develop the transference neurosis with the blank slate therapist. I found that transference is ubiquitous and how it is used is the question. Now I guess I could never be too blank, so I never went along with that. My patients usually stayed in treatment, and they all began in therapy except for two who came for analysis. The others worked their way into analysis so that was how it happened for me. I think most beginners have real conviction in the process which patients pick up on.

So, my first book was about how I worked, I called it 'Deepening the Treatment'—how to do that, how I thought I did it. That was what I tried to address, and it was very popular. It still sells; I still get checks for it which is nice.

MSK: That's impressive.

JH: I just got one the other day. I mean they're not huge but it's nice to know that people are still finding it valuable. It was published in China some years ago and that provided me with many Chinese students. This book is quite different, and I thought the first chapter might explain how I got to thinking this way.

To begin with, I was very lucky in social work school. I had a wonderful internship at a clinic called Greenwich House Counseling Center and it specialized in treating people with drug related problems. They hired me after graduation so that was my first job. Patients didn't have to be junkies or drug addicts; we saw family members; some who used LSD or just marijuana; cocaine and barbiturate users; so, I saw a wide range of patients and I knew nothing. I worked with transvestites, prostitutes, lawyers, professors, a young man who was an exhibitionist, a cocaine addicted air traffic controller (that was scary,); a famous homosexual designer arrested in a public mens' room for lewd behavior addicted to amphetamines and placidil, and sent to my clinic to avoid jail time; a few artists, a middle class college student drug dealer who wanted to be popular and who eventually was able to tell me that his mother sexually abused him, and the list goes on.

I was a beginner, and I learned that connecting came easy to me. I mean I always made friends easily even though I have

131

a shy side. And I have always been curious so one principle I learned in the very beginning of my education by reading the late Ella Freeman Sharpe, was called *benevolent curiosity*. That has been my lodestar. I am naturally curious but *benevolent curiosity* means without criticism, so I found that it worked for me. I didn't even think diagnostically. I just listened and talked to the person in a natural way and this book is pretty much about that. At GHCC one of my first patients —a young man in his late twenties, leaned in and asked me if I could hear the garbage machine in his head. I leaned in, said no and then asked him where he grew up etc. We needed a focus and though his question really threw me, I just sort of did the best I could.

In this book I use the term *leveling the playing field*. That was in stark contrast to the way I was taught. You know the doctor was up there and the patient was down here, and we made the interpretation, and the patient gave the material. I thought, you know, it's infantilizing. It's sort of like the way we treat our students too. I saw analytic work as a partnership rather than me being the all-knowing doctor and they just giving me the material that I would put together. I came up with the phrase 'let's figure it out'. If a patient wanted to quit or was always late, I'd say "let's figure out why. You have a right to do what you want to do, but let's figure out why and then you decide." I saw things as a mystery. Let's figure out this mystery. I think I'm talking too much right now. I want you to ask me some questions.

MSK: I don't have a sense that you are talking too much, not from my angle. I mean you already gave me two major themes and plenty other ideas that I am thinking about, so please just go ahead.

JH: Thanks Sagman—you're easy to talk with.

The ideas expressed in the book are inspired by my patients, my supervisees and their patients, my students, and the vast psychoanalytic literature beginning with Freud and including our most contemporary thinkers.

When I was a student—no computers or PEP-CD Rom—I would spend hours in the New School Library reading the assigned articles. Back then, probably due to an as yet unanalyzed rebelliousness combined with a deep curiosity, I would read a lot of the other articles in the bound volumes, saving the assigned ones for last. In other words, I wandered through the fields "picking up lots of forget-me-nots" (from a song *You Make Me Feel So Young* that Sinatra sang) that I stored away for later use.

Also, before, during, and after formal coursework I was in two long term ongoing seminars with Gertrude Blanck for five years and Martin Bergmann for about seven. I think I'm always learning and of course my patients taught me the most.

Only in the last fifteen years my learning curve changed, and it began with Norman Doidge's book "The Brain that Changes Itself." I reviewed the book—it's about the plasticity of the brain. It gave credence to what I was learning. Norman says "use it or lose it" meaning the new object-analyst is like a new pathway in the brain and as you use that new object and all the experiences that come with it, the old pathway diminishes and becomes a tiny scar—fading away. I see it as involving internalization and new experiences and vistas take over the early ones.

I mention, with immense gratitude, the ideas of the following authors whose contributions, some of them well researched, have made a deep impression: Joseph Sandler, Norman Doidge, Rona Knight, Jaak Panksepp, Sandor Ferenczi, W.R.D. Fairbairn, Ed Tronick, Ella Sharpe, Bernard Berliner, Hans Loewald, and Leonard Shengold. Actually, there are many others too numerous to mention.

I also began questioning Freud who I think was obviously a brilliant man and we wouldn't be here without him probably.

But I think we tended to revere him as though he were a God or something like that. I can look up to people, but not to that degree and I hold on to my right to be curious and even questioning. As an example, I never liked the concept of the Oedipus complex being focal. And the phallo-centric theory that he developed, I took issue with, and I found a few papers who agreed with me so that was nice. I think today in the twenty-first century we pay attention to the mother's influence more and I think so many of my patients all had problematic mothers so that if you want to use only the Oedipus complex it doesn't work. And we must learn about Laius who tried to kill him.

You know if your mother is a problem, and you love your father it's scarier than if you have a nice mother and so I kind of challenged that theory as being central. I think the mother has a huge influence on character and I think most analyses I have conducted or been a part of as a supervisor fit what Ernst Kris called strain trauma as opposed to shock trauma. Shock trauma is if you get raped or something horrible happens once. Strain trauma is ongoing and becomes an undercurrent of a child's life. So, if a child grows up in a what is called a dysfunctional family, he may not be abused physically but the climate that he grows up in is anxiety provoking. PTSD. You never know when the mother is going to blow up or the father is going to come home drunk and angry, those kinds of things. But the mom's helplessness in such cases was as injurious as the dad's abuse.

My patients, pretty much all of them, had such early situations. Even the ones who functioned beautifully. People can function very well but as you go along after a while you realize that they have trouble with relationships. They can be the CEO of a hugely successful company, but they can't really sustain a relationship, especially in marriage or even a real close friendship. They may have superficial friends but because they're always worried unconsciously that whatever happened in childhood is going to happen again with the person they choose, they shy away from developing intimate and deep relationships. Trusting another is frightening.

I think a famous tech-billionaire who is in the headlines nowadays is a perfect example. Here's a guy who had a crazy childhood plus he was a genius so you know you can just look at him and see how his brilliance was compromised by his pathology. His hunger for attention is enormous and I wait for him to crash and burn. His many followers will be devastated because they sort of lived through him. To me it is quite plausible that he wants to go into outer space—that's how far one can go to avoid psychic pain. For good personal and unconscious or split off reasons.

Phillip Bromberg is important in understanding dissociated states.

MSK: That's a good point and let me ask you a question. You already highlighted half a dozen things that catch my ear. There's something when I read your book. It's as though there's a subtle theory of yours that I understand quite well because in some ways it's also very similar to the way I think. It's as if you learn from yourself—like this gentleman and your first patient who was an ex-drug addict. The encounter you described was very touching for some reason.

Now, it is a fact that at that moment in your life you were a very green social worker. The way in which he related to you, and you related to him, feels quite ordinary in our intimate relationships, be it a love relationship or friendship. And perhaps for some good reasons it is something extremely rare in professional relationships.

There is something centrally and deeply human about the way you relate, or "connect" as you would put it. It's not psychoanalytic per se, not a technique or stance but it's a very common, well known, unarticulated interest in humans. A very basic human interest. You know what you said about 'benevolent curiosity' in other discussions we had. In our corporatized world of treatments, it has become a rarity. So, when you were 18 you were talking with your doctor. But that is an anomaly now. It is interesting that as psychoanalytic clinicians, one central function we serve in places like medical schools is to remind, re-teach the young clinicians on how to listen to and talk with patients. A prominent analyst Brian Bird has a book about this—from 70's I believe.

Me and my wife we wrote and presented a draft about this what they call the real relationship versus transference. You know how we subtly demean real relationship and emphasize the transformative power of the transference relationship. It is interesting that when you go back to Freud, and you read his papers on technique very carefully there he talks about a very basic relationship that you kind of mentioned about that curiosity. It is almost like an inborn curiosity we have in others. He calls it effective transference and he says everything is built on that we're curious about others and then you just let it go and then the therapy unfolds

JH: I think the same thing goes in our own analyses, yes, we are our best analyst. I mean the analyst opens certain doors for us. Sometimes we go through them to look at what we may not have considered but I think once we get that idea at least for me that was what happened—we're on our own.

I had three analyses. I started when I was 18 years old, and I didn't know a damn thing about analysis. I had just come home from my honeymoon. I got married when I was 18 and I wasn't very happy. I couldn't sleep, all my friends were at college where I had been planning to go and here, I was at home without any friends and I was not the happiest camper, so I went to my regular doctor. He said go talk to somebody. I remember very well that I said, "well I'm talking to you". I was fresh because he seemed to be rejecting me. He said no go talk to somebody who knows about these things, so I went to my first analyst.

He was nice enough you know, and he pointed to the couch. I said I didn't understand why I should use the couch. I didn't know a thing! I mean I *really* didn't know. And so, I used it and all I could do was look at his ceiling and see all the cracks. I said well you have a terrible ceiling, it is all cracked—why don't you fix that, and I went on like that I mean I didn't know what else to do so. As I look back that had meaning but he didn't pick up on it so that's why right away you know there was stuff there that he missed completely and eventually he let me sit in the chair. Then I would look out the window and talk about the weathervane outside and he thought that was resistance. I was just using what I could see—a weathervane.

Now as I look back, he might have used weather as a metaphor. I was really talking about the weather in my home life when I grew up. We never knew when a hurricane was coming or when it was going to be a sunny weather, so that fed into my character. Being on guard. And here I was talking about the weather, and he didn't pick up on that. And although he was a nice man, I think maybe he thought I wasn't ready to hear it as a metaphor. If a patient of mine was like that I think I'd find a way to share my thoughts. Not as interpretations but as a partner. I might say something like:" Let's see if it has more meaning—like stormy or sunny or rainy" This way I offer my thought, and she can take it or leave it—but she might consider it. I didn't get much in my first analysis. I got the idea that he would listen to me and that he was a nice person, but I didn't really get anything. We couldn't talk with one another; he couldn't read me. We couldn't be on each other's wavelength so to speak. On the other hand, he was there for me and that was very important.

He was into the Oedipus complex, and though I adored my father because he was the steady one in the house, and he loved me, my mother didn't. She never wanted kids and so I had a skewed family. I don't impose the Oedipus myth that Freud chose though of course it had a place. Narcissus was a better myth I think that he should have explored more. Oedipus's parents abandoned him as a baby—and Freud never focusses on that. Child abuse and neglect goes on today way more than we like to face. Statistics are horrifying and they only count physical abuse.

MSK: I honestly think they're interpreting the myth of Oedipus Rex quite partially. As an example, they don't understand the seduction of the mother in Oedipus. I think it can be interpreted in many different ways and that the dominant interpretation is I think very partial.

JH: Jocasta and the Laius father both let their baby go and left him on the mountain. I mean maybe in those days that was customary but in Freud's Vienna you didn't do that. The other thing that I must mention is I got very interested in child development which I think he saw only through the psychosexual phases. I mean he had the oral, anal, phallic phases and all that stuff. OK that's interesting but I think he missed how a child developed—how the brain is formed. Not long ago I got very interested in David Eagleman's podcast on the brain. At the same time, I was very inspired by Norman Doidge who talked about the brain's plasticity. The Freud I learned was into drives and death instinct and with Anna the defenses that were to be analyzed. I don't know what else to say. They impressed me but so much more has happened with neuroscience, and we must incorporate it. Tronick has given me so much to think about.

MSK: I feel like I have a question that is coming to mind as we speak Jane. You seem to have kept a rebellious and independent spirit alive. Was it hidden or were you able to talk about this in the analysis or with some others?

JH: I'm rebellious in that I don't buy everything that I'm fed. If I don't get it, I'll search more. I won't just be a 'good' student all the time. As I told you before it is easy to define me as a "good, warm" person. And that is probably true about me. But I am not a "goody two shoes" at all. I've analyzed that but Hartmann talked about 'change in function' and although I've forgotten it exactly, maybe it applies too. The ego somehow changes the instincts into higher level activities.

When I was a student, we didn't have computers, so we had to go to the library to do our reading and the journals were in these big bound volumes. I would go and I would read everything else before the assigned literature. I learned a lot that way. I would just read an article, and I said that's interesting. I would just flip through a journal and read all the articles that caught my attention so that was a rebellious thing I think in my character. Someone I used to know said it had to do with the primal scene—maybe so but so what?

MSK: How did you read them? I have the fantasy that it was a secret relationship you had outside of the confines of the institute one may say.

JH: I don't know I would read the International Journal, or any journal and they were all in this big bound volume so I would just open a page, and I would find an article and I would read it. I didn't discuss it I just thought about it and went on.

MSK: You thought about it on your own.

JH: Yes of course. I don't know how I can explain it. There are many angles—wanting to know more... being competitive—being hungry—I would read about techniques, and I would read about other theories, and I don't remember what I read—this was a long time ago, but I can say it was an absorbing interest. And sure, I can relate this to my mother who probably had a mood disorder which scared me and also angered me.

MSK: You took the reading seriously it's not like you did it read it for the sake of reading it.

JH: Took it very seriously, would spend hours at the library.

MSK: You gave serious attention to it, so you secretly had more teachers you were talking with. That was secretive and rebellious and here I use rebellion in a creative way. To me it seems that during those times you don't say your criticisms, disagreements out loud, right? They would treat you as a heretic of sorts I assume.

JH: Of course. In school I went along with the line in the program and uh I think today students they're a little different. The manners were different before the sixties. We didn't challenge the teacher, but I mean we would talk together in the elevator after class. That spirit of not challenging the authority still persists as a powerful undertone. But that is a whole other topic, and it's still the same way about diagnosis. I believe that to give a patient a diagnosis like in the DSM diagnosis, you see through that lens of borderline or obsessive, you know whatever they have in there. I can understand that could be helpful, but you'll miss other things when you put a person into a box no matter how hard you try. Nancy McWilliams has written beautifully about how helpful it is—but it does a disservice to a patient for me. What one can learn in diagnosis is often true, but a sensitive therapist will know intuitively, I think. Kohut did give us good advice about working with the narcissistic patient which is always frustrating and often impossible.

MSK: After many years I understood the following. In a session if I start thinking about diagnosis and theory, I am as a rule, feeling stuck. That is when diagnosis and theory emerge as a preoccupation in my thoughts. One may say I'm calling some higher powers, diagnosis, my teachers or Freud for help So I take it as diagnostic of my situation that I am confused or feel stuck.

Jane, I can't fully articulate this, but it is as if we think similarly, there's a common trend here. I think you're an eternal apprentice in the work. You learn from the patient and the way you work as a dyad. Thus, a main teacher becomes you, Jane Hall in relation to the patient. Of course, theory is very helpful but if you start with the theory and go to a patient then I think you'll lose the experience you are immersed in. If you go from the experience to theory than you are in terra firma. Sullivan named this as participant observer, but I believe we can add another word participant observer thinker. Something like that.

With this stance, in my opinion you avoid becoming self-psychologist or object relationist or one of many such schools. But you become who you are, and I think we, at the bottom, are at our best when we are our ordinary professional selves. And that defies any school of psychoanalysis.

JH: Agree fully. I was lucky to study with Martin Bergmann for years. He used to say 'Even if you don't like an article or you don't agree with the author, you learn something. Every article has something of value' and that to me is an open mind. We need to have more open minds. You know how they argue at meetings; I wonder why they can't say *"tell me more about that. I just need to hear, let me think about it let me consider it. I don't usually think that way but it's interesting let me think about it".* Instead of just knocking it down. There's so much nastiness in this field, have you picked that up?

MSK: Yeah, we're like political parties.

JH: How can we believe in analysis if we're so nasty to each other. What kind of analysis have people had? I mean the narcissism is unbelievable. And I don't think you can really help that much, a real narcissist is very difficult to treat, if they decide to come to treatment, which is rare in itself. I mean I supervise several people who have narcissistic patients and it's really difficult for them...and me.

MSK: I think one of the wonderful things about your book is you make how you are with and work with the patient very clear. Jane Hall appears as a therapist as a unique individual and thinker and a clinician so that's really very generous of you for the interested reader. You manage to not hide behind jargon and heavy words but say 'this is how I think about it, and this is what I do with it'.

JH: Maybe I can end by saying I think we do not remember enough that everybody is unique. You just said, unique in the way we connect. I mean one person will connect with you differently than with me, so the dyad creates a unique body you know—I use the word uniquity—I made that up I think—I don't know if that's a word. And that's how jazz music came into this book because the jazz musician will play something differently every time. Every performance is unique and even the same song they'll play it differently; they're free to improvise.

MSK: I like your concept of "uniquity". It is wonderfully apt and creative.

JH: Thank you, Sagman, for talking with me—you made it fun and comfortable. I'd like to add one idea that really impressed me from Warren Poland—he speaks of "Witnessing" and I think this an incredibly useful concept that no one seems to talk about. So, I end by recommending his paper.

Responses to the Contributors

Jane Hall

I begin my response to the interesting reactions to the *Power of Connection* by expressing my gratitude to Sagman, who is now the editor in chief of this unique online journal, IJCD, and to Arnie Richards for creating it.

Controversy is important in our profession—especially when we are able to be open minded. Instead of just plain disagreement, I have suggested prefacing our reactions with a phrase like "I never thought about that, can you tell me more?" or "Let me give your idea some thought."

As a beginning student in the 1970s I remember attending many 'scientific' meetings filled with a hostility that I found truly cringeworthy. "Why such hostility" would make an interesting paper. Analysts who were invited to give papers were too often ruthlessly challenged—even Winnicott who suffered a heart attack not long after his rude reception at NYPSI, or so the story goes. And Bion's reception in Los Angeles, in the book of transcribed lectures, (Wilfred Bion: Los Angeles Seminars and Supervision 2013) was not what I would call warm.

Things are better these days, but I admit to fearing the publication of this book for it challenges certain concepts and introduces an analyst who works with and not on a patient by using a "let's figure it out" approach.

Here, in this journal, no one challenged this approach which goes against all that I was originally taught in the 1970s and 80s. In the book I tried to bring us down to earth, to be real, to focus on what we call the working alliance in simple language. I suggested using the transference as clues but not lingering in it as I was schooled to do.

My major idea was creating a level playing field with both partners in the dyad working as a team in order to solve mysteries by using the phrase "Let's figure it out." This approach honors the working alliance alongside the transference. Transference is useful as a clue because it illuminates what caused mal-adaptations, symptoms, and character styles. I have seen that allowing intense transference to build for long periods can take over one's treatment running the risk of engraving memories and perceptions of childhood relationships more deeply in the brain.

Ed Tronick's work along with Norman Doidge's book *The Brain that Changes Itself* deepened my thinking in the last twenty-five years and along with Rona Knight's research on development, inspired this book. Ella Sharpe and Leonard Shengold were with me from the start, so benevolent curiosity and caritas became my north stars. I now think I would have been more comfortable with Sandor Ferenczi's voice and ideas, but I found him later. I was a bit disappointed that the generous and well thought through responses seemed to avoid arguing these ideas. But on the other hand, they taught me so much.

I will start my responses with the last chapter, based on interviews with Martin Bergmann, so beautifully discussed by Daniel Benveniste who begins by saying he had always wanted to meet Martin.

He goes on to introduce us to his mentor, Nathan Adler and from there he mentions Siegfried Bernfeld, one of my favorites. Thank you, Daniel, for prompting me to re-read Bernfeld's classic paper in which he expresses his dissatisfaction with how psychoanalysis is taught. He bemoans the fact that with the impressive growth of institutes over thirty plus years, nothing had changed since the 'teacher centered' Eitingon model had been adopted. On Psychoanalytic Training (1962). Psychoanal. Q., (31):453–482. Sixty-three years later things are still pretty much the same although we do honor a relational model. I would go further by saying that our clinical work reflects the teaching model because we cannot seem to help imposing theory on the patient. I think this happens when we attach ourselves to only one theory.

Daniel speaks of our many theories as lenses through which we see our patients, agreeing with Martin's advice to learn our original theory well and also as many others as possible. I would go farther. I think of chewing up these ideas we learn and digesting them so that they become part of us. For instance, it must eventually become natural to mirror the easily injured patient and not a mechanical reaching for Kohut. Instead, we tend to idealize certain theoreticians and although understandable, it may be why psychoanalysis is in trouble.

Idealization is a major problem when it prevents us from thinking on our own. Our need for authority has never been resolved and taken to the extreme this explains today's world. The craving for authority has always been an undercurrent or even an unconscious wish in our field as much as we protest. Like the real world, psychoanalytic work can feel dangerous and we either deny our fear by becoming a self-psychologist or by mastering it. Theories must not serve as crutches; they must be authentically used. And we can and should feel free to be ourselves nurtured by digesting what we learn. Daniel's contribution includes in my mind the history of our dilemma: the Laius Complex. Why indeed do we focus on poor Oedipus without emphasizing his paranoid dad, Laius who left him on a mountain to die. And we mustn't forget Jocasta's compliance. Freud based his theory on what he saw as the child's wish to sexually conquer the parent of the opposite sex. But in doing so he avoided the parents' jealousy of the child. Not many analysts go along with this. It occurs to me that as we rightly blame Trump and Elon for their attempts to kill democracy, we rarely look to their abusive fathers who caused these men to seek vengeance.

Daniel has given me so much to think about. Freud and his followers wanted to make psychoanalysis a respected science and, in my mind, the humanistic approach suffered. We rarely hear Leo Stone or Warren Poland, or other humanists quoted—at least I don't. There are many things we don't know, and we have so much to learn. I thank Daniel for understanding that love has an important place in the student–teacher relationship. Martin knew that and I know he was loved by his students. I'm sure this inspired him.

Sagman's reaction to chapter one makes me confident that we are in agreement about love's place in our work. Most analysts shy away from using that word and even bristle at the concept. So, I can only thank him for 'getting' and even liking the chapter.

Rona Knight has presented us with her important research that makes us rethink our picture of child development as taking place in specific phases or stages. She shows us that we are always developing and that it's never too late to accomplish important developmental steps. Many adults have not individuated enough to see 'the other' and come to therapy because this failure prevents them from fulfilling relationships. Analytic work can help with this developmental step. Separation anxiety plagues many adults and when the dyad sees this come alive in treatment, analytic work can diminish it. I had never been taught the non-linear dynamic systems theory Rona uses and her explanation is appreciated. Her contribution to our work needs traction and focus. I end this appreciation with her words. "Our job then becomes one of helping change our patient's story about him or herself by helping them reflect on what is preventing them from flexibly adapting to present and future developmental fluidity and reorganization. In this way, we can co-create a new narrative that promotes transformation and a more flexible and resilient development."

Jon Allen's ideas are similar to mine. I thank him for taking the time to share his thoughts and hope I hear his music someday.

Thank you, David Cooper, for your suggestions and the way you phrased them. I agree that 'self-murder' and 'bad enough object' are iffy attempts to describe what I'm trying to convey. I think my play on Winnicott's good enough object by using bad enough was not helpful, necessary, and might be seen by some as rude although I hold Winnicott in high esteem. What I meant was the mother who confuses the child by erratic behavior; a mother who is highly ambivalent about being a mother; a mother who may or may not be evil but who damages her child psychologically by her incapacity to show affection; a mother who is capable of providing the necessities but does not feel the love the child needs. The cold, anxious mother who unconsciously wishes to kill the child due to her own deprivations and trauma. Even these words are not capturing what I mean because a multitude of feelings are often condensed. A hatred grows between the mother-daughter couple due to narcissistic injuries that bounce back and forth. Suicidal thoughts are often wishes to kill this internalized mother, hence self-murder because self and object differentiation has not been accomplished. I think of Sylvia Plath. Who was she killing? And was she doing to her children what had been done to her?

But David, I think we agree basically, and I will try to make my language reflect my thoughts better. As for splitting, I think dissociating may be what I mean—or even suppressing. I'm not keen on pinning things down because one can't really know and labels box us in. This may be muddying the waters, but I think we have multiple selves that are called forth by outside events whether they be positive or negative. The cohesive self was never a convincing concept for me although we usually present ourselves this way in social situations. We all hear about or even know well known and successful people who behind the scenes are living perverse lives, who behave sadistically, and who sometimes aren't at all aware of these selves. We might see this as psychotic but really, what is it that allows these folks to see themselves as normal. Extreme narcissism could explain it, but it remains baffling to me. An inability to recognize 'the other' seems apt. These individuals live by projecting. So far different selves or maybe self-states are more accurate. I have to re-read Bromberg.

I have never met Todd Dean, but I have read his interesting contributions to the members list. His messages didn't always appeal to me—sometimes I just didn't get what he was talking about. BUT I do like that he is an original thinker and probably somewhat of a rebel. His reaction to my words was spot on for me because I absolutely agree that words are representative of thoughts, can never really capture them, and almost always change them. We all do our best and the words we choose are ones we hope will resonate to the unique patient/ partner. I admit that the structural model drilled into me so long ago is hard to shake, at least in thinking of defenses and self-esteem. As for having enough information to know the truth, I don't think I said that. I don't even think there is one truth. We seek it but like reality, it is different from one moment to the next depending on perspective, mood, hormone levels, lack of sleep, diet, which side of the bed you get up on to name but a few. We have a picture of normality that IMO is different for everyone for it involves large doses of projection.

Francisco, I can't possibly take on all your points—there are so many. I do believe in corrective emotional experiences as part of our work. Spending twenty years with Lisa (chapter 8) convinced me. You can call it any number of things like identification, internalization, influence of a new object etc.

but just because eighty years ago Alexander introduced it and was attacked vigorously, I see no reason to abandon the concept. I believe that in everyday life we have corrective emotional experiences unless we live in a cave.

Lisa grew tremendously in so many ways, and I attribute that growth to our connection. The analyst is who the patient needs and only towards the end is she allowed to be an individuated other.

Open your eyes to what so often happens before and after vacations. Such times are extremely painful for many patients, who, as a result, often want to end treatment. My interventions, my expertise was far less important than my staying power in allowing her to grow. It was our combined willingness and mostly unconscious staying power on a very long journey and our unconscious and sometimes conscious efforts to keep going mattered. So, whether you like my use of ego strengths or my understanding of countertransference, I feel pretty good about much of my work.

And yes, like Freud, I think love and work are supremely important measures of a satisfying life. And yes, holding and enjoying a job after losing many is a sign of progress. I am truly sorry that you, Francisco, couldn't see anything psychoanalytic in the vignette about Bill. Obviously, we have different understandings of the work we do. Granted it was a brief sketch, but I felt the outline of our work illustrated that sometimes just being there without intruding is healing. My stance was listening and even witnessing empathically.

You might want to read Warren Poland's work on witnessing. Bill's long-standing disappointment needed expression. Letting go with his tears had never happened and it showed him a side of himself here-tofore unacceptable. In this case a quiet, accepting analyst was appropriate because he knew a lot from his former analyst who seemed to lack the ability to listen. In fact, when all is said and done, I think our many theories and concepts, my own included, are meant to keep us going and that our caritas matters most.

149

Next, I want to thank Fred Gioia and Lance Dodes for 'getting me'—for seeing what I was aiming at and for doing this so movingly. It's a wonderful feeling to be understood—especially when what you're trying to articulate requires courage and daring. The evolution of depth psychotherapy is ongoing but when so many in the field are so quick to say scornfully "that's not psychoanalysis," it's daunting. So, when I read what Fred Gioia and Lance Dodes contributed, I think I experienced a corrective emotional experience.

Lance has a valid point about my interjecting thoughts on the brain, but I'd like to explain why I did. First of all, I was struck by Doidge's work on brain plasticity and because in my semi-retirement I spend a fair amount of time getting lost on the internet, one day I came across a brilliant and likable guy, David Eagleman, who can be found on YouTube or on his podcast called Inner Cosmos. He really captures my attention with his scientific explanations of what happens in the brain, and this blended with Norman Doidge's influence. I do wish he would talk about our work but perhaps not. Maybe he and Doidge could talk—he often has guests. Together they had a major impact on my thinking about the plasticity of the brain with convincing examples. I don't think we really know where the mind is, but I do find the brain fascinating. Fred, I've never met you, but your praise will stay with me always.

Luba Kessler is a beautiful writer, and her contributions always add depth to conversations. Bringing Rousseau and ethnology into her response elevates our thinking. She got me thinking about the analyst's (or anyone's) ability to enter a story. Is it our fluid boundaries or is it our willingness to let go of ourselves just enough to really be with someone else? However, this capacity is not without risks. The pull of a good story can throw one off balance, so the analyst has the chore of not forgetting her purpose. Entering another's story is both an asset and a liability. And this ability strengthens with experience. In the beginning of our journeys maintaining balance usually requires assistance, hence supervision or case discussion. Like swimming in deep waters, the beginner might benefit from a life vest. The powerful undertow of a story can cause the enactments that teach us so much if we recognize them. At times consultation is useful because getting swept away can cause a certain blindness or countertransference. Freud suggested analysis every five years but today with such long analyses, that may be unnecessary. I like the idea of a combination of analysis and supervision that is so frowned upon and I never explored why that idea is taboo. How often do we take sides with a character in a story—maybe the hero or even the villain? This tendency gets in the way of what I mean by neutrality. A patient often presents a parent as horrible but as treatment deepens, good aspects of that parent surface. We therapists must be careful of taking sides. On the other hand, when real abuse has occurred it requires empathy. I mentioned in the introduction of this book a great paper by Purcell who speaks of being with a patient in "non-meaning" as well as in symbolic communication. Experience and even common-sense help. Listening to and tolerating Avant garde music requires both effort and relaxation in order to enjoy it, for me anyway. Is this akin to listening to a psychotic type of free association?

Luba asks what motivates curiosity and I wonder too. The stock answer is the primal scene, but I think it's much more. Children need encouragement and safety to explore and that makes sense to me. Analytic work involves exploring and it comes easier to some than to others.

But as long as it remains benign or benevolent curiosity is necessary in doing psychoanalytic work. Luba reminds us that each analyst grows by joining her patient/partner on their journeys just as when we visit other cultures. I believe that experiencing what we are not used to strengthens us. A sense of adventure is helpful—even necessary to travel with someone we don't know, so the drive to connect helps.

I end these responses to those who took the time to critique these chapters by saying thank you. Arnie Richards's idea is original in that it provides, in one space, a look at how people think about each other's ideas and hopefully grow through discussion. I know I did, and I shall be eternally grateful to all.

———

Psychoanalytic History—Sketches

Mark F. Poster

Abstract:

Intersubjectivity in various guises (unconscious communication, transference/countertransference interaction, reciprocal free association, mutual enactment, interpersonal, relational and field theory) is the coin of the contemporary psychoanalytic world, even while evidence-based therapy (EBT) is the coin of the health care marketplace. This paper explores the role of Sandor Ferenczi both in the early development of intersubjectivity and also in the utraquistic (see below) bridging between the domains of science and humanism. Ferenczi courageously pursued his own clinical research and writing even when criticized by Freud and his followers, of whom he was among the closest to Freud over several decades.

Keywords: dialogue of the unconsciouses, intersubjectivity, mutuality, utraquism

A kluger farshtait fun ain vort tsvai
A wise man hears one word and understands two
(Yiddish expression)

153

Intersubjectivity in history:

Intersubjectivity concerns a subject or a self-embedded in interaction. Freud's mental agencies, on the other hand, were more objective and about an individual.

The concept of intersubjectivity originated in philosophy. Names like Husserl, Heidegger, Buber and Binswanger are associated with it. Merleau-Ponty (1968) and Kraus and Derrida (2004) used the term "invagination" to describe a dynamic differentiation between the self and the other dating back to Kant's *Critique of Judgment*. Detailed histories of intersubjectivity in psychoanalysis (Thompson, Kirshner) trace its roots to German phenomenology (Hegel), French linguistics (Lacan) and a combination of both of these (Laing). Ferenczi's "dialogue of the unconsciouses" is an important milestone in the development of intersubjectivity in psychoanalysis.

Binaries and *utraquism*:

Psychoanalysis sprang from a cultural environment on two continents suffused with mysticism and religious movements, including Transcendentalism, Emmanuelism, and Christian Science. Sandor Ferenczi (1873–1933) was writing about Spiritism (1899) before he ever met Sigmund Freud in 1908. William James published a paper entitled "A Suggestion about Mysticism" in 1910, one year after his walk with Freud from Clark University to the then new Union Station in Worcester, Massachusetts. After joining Freud on that same visit to America in 1909 and writing outlines for Freud's contemporaneous talks, Ferenczi returned to Europe and visited the Berlin psychic Frau Seidler. Ferenczi wrote to Freud on November 11, 1910, that he was "a great soothsayer... I am reading my patients' thoughts (in my free associations). The future methodology of psychoanalysis must make use of this." (Freud and Ferenczi, 1993, p. 235).

The tension (within the friendship) between Freud and Ferenczi over many years is emblematic of a tension in medicine (and especially in the mental health disciplines) between science and humanities. These categories were described by Dilthey (1907/2010) as *naturwissenschaften* and *geisteswissenschaften*. The former uses the method of *erklaren* (nomothetic or law-governed explanations). The latter uses the method of *verstehen* (idiographic interpretations of meaning, sometimes called hermeneutics). Aron and Starr (2015) warned that these domains are not complete binaries. In fact, Freud, the objectivist, was also interested in what he termed "thought transference". He just wanted his interest kept secret so as not to delegitimize the reputation of psychoanalysis as a science. And Ferenczi was nothing if not empirical in his serial experiments in activity, elasticity, relaxation and mutuality. Ferenczi was motivated and guided by feeling his way into helping the individual patient in front of him.

Intersubjectivity requires a bridge to the wider world of mental health treatment. Ferenczi (1933) called such a bridge between science and psychology *"utraquistic"*. *Utraquism* comes from the Latin *sub utraque specie* meaning "in both kinds", or as Joni Mitchell sang "from both sides now". *Utraquism* in the Christian church meant that both the bread and wine should be served in the Eucharist sacrament and to all the laity, not just the priests. Ferenczi, perhaps uniquely, bridged the ideas of Janet, Jung and Freud (Cassullo).

Ackerman (2017) creatively compared psychoanalysis to a voyage at sea. She explored Freud's resistance to Rolland's "oceanic feeling", seeing in it mortal dangers, an expression of the death instinct that Freud wrote about. Yet Rolland's own "oceanic" experience gave him a feeling of expansiveness and "vital renewal". Ackerman then uses Melville's novel *Moby Dick* to further explore this difference in response to going to sea in all its metaphors- e.g. the uncanny, the unconscious, birth, bonding, danger, and death. She contrasts Captain Ahab's "monomaniacal goal" of killing the great white whale Moby Dick with Ishmael's contemplative meditation from the ship's masthead. Again, without falling into a false binary, it is not hard to see Captain Ahab in Freud, the Conquistador, determined to plumb the secrets of nature (Barron et al). In like manner, Ferenczi, like Ishmael, is more open to feelings and to adapting himself to the wider world including difficult patients on their own terms.

Dialogue of the unconsciouses:

Ferenczi coined the term "dialogue of the unconscious" in 1910 when he treated a 24-year-old man for impotence. The patient lived with his widowed mother who accompanied him to Ferenczi's office. He spoke in two voices, a high soprano and a baritone. Ferenczi understood the soprano voice to be an unconscious communication between the young man and his mother that was used as a "prohibition of the incestuousness". Other manifest symptoms were bedwetting, a phobia of mice, and cross-dressing for entertainment. A second similar case in a 17-year-old was seen by Ferenczi in 1914. He wrote both cases up in a paper published in 1915. The title was *Psychogenic Anomalies of Voice Production*. Ferenczi wrote, "This is one of the so frequent cases which I call the "dialogue of the unconscious," where the unconscious of two persons fully understand each other, without the consciousness of either having any inkling of it." (Ferenczi, 1915, p. 28).

Years later, on 12 April 1932, Ferenczi noted in his *Clinical Diary* that the idea of a "dialogue of the unconsciouses" (now used in the plural to emphasize that two people were involved) had been "launched if I remember correctly, by me". Here is how Ferenczi described this dialogue—"When two people converse, not only a conscious dialogue takes place but an unconscious one, from both sides. In other words, next to the attention-cathected conversation, or parallel to it, a relaxed dialogue is also pursued." (Ferenczi, 1932, p. 84).

Schismatic year and paradigm shift in psychoanalysis:

1923–24 was a "schismatic" year resulting in a "paradigm shift in psychoanalysis". (Bokay; Rudnytsky, 2002, p. 141;

Hoffer, P.; Poster, 2009, p. 197) In that year, Freud wrote *The Ego and the Id* which was the beginning of ego psychology. In the same year, 1923, Georg Groddeck, a German physician who had befriended Freud in 1917 by writing letters to him, wrote a book of letters, *The Book of the It*, which English professor and psychoanalyst, Peter Rudnytsky, described as "the greatest masterpiece of psychoanalytic literature". (Rudnytsky, 2002, p.163) In 1924, on commission by Freud to combine psychoanalytic theory with practice, Ferenczi and Otto Rank wrote *The Development of Psychoanalysis* which emphasized *erlebnis* (experience) in the here-and-now, rather than remembering. Thus began the schism between objective ego psychology and experiential, later relational, psychoanalysis.

Groddeck used what he called *Das* Es, or the It, to described "an undefinable force we are all lived by." Groddeck had adapted the concept *Das Es* from Carl Gustav Carus (1789–1869) and *Naturphilosophie*. (Balenci) *Groddeck* listened intently for this force in his patients to "whisper" to his own *Das Es* to try to understand his patients, and especially their physical symptoms. This intersubjective treatment technique was very similar to Ferenczi's clinical use of his concept of "dialogue of the unconsciouses". Freud recognized the similarity in "artistico-intuitive" style and predilection for the occult of both Ferenczi and Groddeck. In addition, Ferenczi had numerous physical symptoms, and Groddeck was very successful at curing them. Accordingly, Freud immediately introduced Ferenczi to Groddeck. They became lifelong friends. (Poster, 2009) Groddeck helped Ferenczi separate from Freud's "crushing paternalism" and find his own voice. (Fortune, p. 92).

Freud (following Plato and Heinroth) adapted Groddeck's *Das Es* to be the wild Id of his tripartite model. (Poster, 1997) Groddeck wrote to his wife on May 15, 1923, that Freud "disregards the constructive aspect of my It (*Das Es*)." (Groddeck, 1977, p. 13) "Since Freud revised and narrowed the scope of Groddeck's It (*Das Es*), later psychoanalytic theories were generated to fill the experiential void." (Poster et al, 2016, p. 172). Nevertheless, some Freud scholars claim that the interpersonal was "always implicit" (Lothane, 1997) in Freud's work, and that Freud was already an inter-subjectivist before he "lost sight of the intersubjective when he tried to locate and date the origin of sexual drives within the individual." (House).

Ferenczi had his own *utraquistic* ideas that he termed "bio-analysis" and, with Elizabeth Severn, an *Orpha* that he described as "an omnipotent intelligence...an *ad hoc* tele-plastic organ (that)...tracked me down to be of service to her." (Ferenczi, 1933, p. 121) According to Galina Hristeva, "*Orpha*—who is definitely of the same origin as Groddeck's *Das Es*—is only a fragment and thus lacks the totality and monumental indivisibility typical of Groddeck's concept. Ferenczi places a stronger accent on the fragmentation but still preserves the connection to the big Whole, to the *Weltseele* (World-soul)—or from his historic perspective to the "protopsyche". The *Weltseele* is a dynamic and creative forming principle in the universe. Being a productive, "indefatigable" force, the *Weltseele* does not cease to be active in each fragment. It is also active both in the analysand and the analyst. Besides, fragmentation allows for more creativity and freedom when re-structuring the individual soul and its links to the *Weltseele* after trauma and a catastrophe. Because of our kinship to the World-Soul we are able to participate in cosmic forces, in the Universal Soul of the World, the *Weltseele*. *Orpha* is a "supra-individual" entity (Ferenczi, 1932, p. 13) precisely due to her connection to the World-Soul. (Hristeva, 2019, 529–530).

Such a mystical force would be very foreign to Freud. Freud did, however, recommend in 1912 that the analyst "must bend his own unconscious like a receptive organ to the transmitting unconscious of the patient". And in 1915 Freud noted, "It is a very remarkable thing that the unconscious of one human being can react upon that of the other, without passing through the conscious mind." Note that the quote above from Freud about unconscious communication is from the same year—1915—that Ferenczi had published a report of two cases and coined the term "dialogue of the unconscious".

Mutual analysis:

Much like Ferenczi, Groddeck wrote to Freud in June 1917, "Everything with me ultimately gets channeled into the treatment of patients." (Groddeck, 1977, p. 40).

Ferenczi experimented with mutual analysis with both Georg Groddeck and then Elizabeth Severn. While this experiment was considered to be successful by and for both Ferenczi and Severn, Ferenczi advised, "Mutual analysis: only a last resort!" (Ferenczi, 1932, p. 115) The mutual analysis between Ferenczi and Severn is described by Peter Rudnytsky as "the paradigm for the contemporary shift to a two-person conceptualization of clinical work, just as Freud's self-analysis was paradigmatic for the one-person perspective of classical theory. Both of these epochal events are paradoxically at once unique and unrepeatable foundational acts of psychoanalysis..." (Rudnytsky, 2022, p. 8) Mutual analysis was also "the fountainhead of self-psychology as well as of relational psychoanalysis." (Rudnytsky, 2022, p. 15).

Two-person psychoanalysis:

In one of his very last papers, Freud (1938) stated in a matter-of-fact manner, "But at this point we are reminded that the work of analysis consists of two quite different portions, that it is carried on in two separate localities, that *it involves two people,* to each of whom a distinct task is assigned. It may for a moment seem strange that such a fundamental fact should not have been pointed out long ago; but it will immediately be perceived that there was nothing being kept back in this, that *it is a fact which is universally known and, as it were, self-evident...*" (italics added). Notwithstanding the above statement, Freud's emphasis throughout his career had been on a one-person interpretive technique.

Following up on his landmark book with Rank (1924), Ferenczi "developed his conception of the transference-countertransference interaction, understood not only as a therapeutic instrument, but as the central kernel of the analytic work" (Cabre). Among the many two-person psychoanalytic theories that followed are countertransference identification with "intuitive... (and) complementary attitude" (Deutsch, H.), interpersonal psychiatry (Sullivan), listening with a third ear (Reik), countertransference as unconscious perception (Heimann), concordant and complementary countertransference (Racker), projective counter- identification (Grinberg), reciprocal free association (Isakower), intersubjectivity (Lacan), role responsiveness (Sandler), a child with a mother (Mahler, Winnicott, Stern, Beebe), countertransference and mutual enactments (Jacobs, Renik), affective engagement at the intimate edge (Ehrenberg), interpsychic communication (Bolognini), implicit knowing (BPCSG), the analytic third (Ogden), complexity theory (Galatzer-Levy), field theory (Barangers, Ferro), intersubjective systems theory (Stolorow), reciprocal recognition (Benjamin), intersubjective ego psychology (Chodorow), dramatology (Lothane, 2009), intersubjective Bionian theory (Brown), and more (Bohleber). Beyond these examples of theories of two-person, or intersubjective, psychoanalysis, more will be described. Indeed, as Arnold Modell has said (personal communication), "The possibilities for what two people can say to each other in a room are almost infinite."

The paradigm shift to two-person psychoanalysis was begun with Ferenczi's "dialogue of the unconsciouses" and is complete. Indeed, it is likely that all analysts today consider themselves to be "two-person" psychoanalysts. While some relational psychoanalysts still refer disparagingly to "one-person, classical analysts", I have yet to hear anyone identify themselves as such. Yet, evidence-based, short-term therapy remains the standard used by third-party payers. While minimally effective in drug-like studies measured against placebo, such treatments have low rates of compliance and low long-term efficacy in naturalistic settings. (Shedler).

Conclusion:

Ferenczi was a classical and contemporary psychoanalyst (Borgogno). He was a pioneer of trauma treatment (Bonomi), object relations and mutuality (Haynal), and an "ancestor" of the relational movement (Harris and Kuchuk). Ferenczi viewed mutual analysis as a technique of "last resort". Nevertheless, Peter Rudnytsky (personal communication) considers Freud's self-analysis and Ferenczi and Severn's mutual analysis to be "the iconic twin foundational pillars in the history of psychoanalysis". Ferenczi's "dialogue of the unconsciouses" was an important milestone on the road to the now prevalent psychoanalytic modes and schools of intersubjectivity. It is also an *utraquistic* bridge between the science of evidence-based psychotherapy and the humanism of intersubjective models of psychoanalysis.

References

Ackerman, S. (2017). Exploring Freud's resistance to the oceanic feeling. *Journal of the American Psychoanalytic Association*, 65 (1): 9–31.

Aron, L. and Starr, K. Freud and Ferenczi, wandering Jews in Palermo, in Harris, A. and Kuchuk, S., eds. (2015). *The Legacy of Sandor Ferenczi*, London: Routledge.

Atwood, G.E. and Stolorow, R.D. (2014). *Structures of Subjectivity: Explorations in Psychoanalytic Phenomenology and Contextualism*, London: Routledge.

Balenci, M. (2021). Jung's and Groddeck's analytic practice: Alternative methods that have prevailed over Freud's psychoanalysis. *International Journal of Jungian Studies*, 7(4): 1–27.

Baranger, M. & Baranger, W. (1961–62). The analytic situation as a dynamic field. *International Journal of Psychoanalysis*, 2008, 89: 795–826.

Barron, J.W., Beaumont, R., Goldsmith, G.N., Good, M.I., Pyles, R.L., Rizzuto, A. and Smith, H.F. (1991). Sigmund Freud: The Secrets of Nature and the Nature of Secrets. *International Review of Psychoanalysis*, 18: 143–163.

Beebe, B. and Lachmann, F.M. (2014). *The Origins of Attachment*, New York: Routledge.

Benjamin, J. (2004). Beyond doer and done to: An intersubjective view of thirdness. *Psychoanalytic Quarterly,* 73: 5–46.

Bohleber, W. (2013). The concept of intersubjectivity in psychoanalysis: Taking Critical Stock. *International Journal of Psychoanalysis*, 94 (4): 799–823.

Bokay, A. (1998). Turn of fortune in psychoanalysis: The 1924 Rank debates and the origins of hermeneutic psychoanalysis. *International Forum of Psychoanalysis,* 7(4): 189–199.

Bolognini, S. (2004). Intrapsychic-interpsychic. *International Journal of Psychoanalysis,* 85 (2): 337–358.

Bonomi, C. Ferenczi: Heir of Freud and Dissident. A Personal View, paper presented in Florence, Italy, May 3, 2018.

Borgogno, F. (2019). Sandor Ferenczi, a classical and contemporary psychoanalyst: (with particular reference to transference and countertransference). *American Journal of Psychoanalysis,* 79: 453–467.

Boston Change Process Study Group (BCPSG) (2007). The Foundational Level of Psychodynamic Meaning. *International Journal of Psychoanalysis*, 88 (4): 843–860.

Brown, L. (2011). *Intersubjective processes and the unconscious: An integration of Freudian, Kleinian and Bionian perspectives,* London: Routledge.

Cabre, L.J.M. (2022). The Freud-Ferenczi Dialogue after the Formulation of the Second Topic. *American Journal of Psychoanalysis,* 82 (2): 222–232.

Cassullo, G. "Ferenczi's 'Confusion of Tongues' as a Bridge between Janet and Freud, paper presented in Florence, Italy, May 5, 2018.

Chodorow, N.J. (2004). The American independent tradition: Loewald, Erikson, and the (possible) rise of intersubjective ego psychology. *Psychoanalytic Dialogues,* 14: 207–232.

Deutsch, H. (1926). Occult events during psychoanalysis. *Imago,* 12 (2–3): 418–433.

Dilthey, W. (2010). *Selected Works, Volume III: The Formation of the Historical World in the Human Sciences,* Makkreel, R.A. and Frithjof, R. (eds.), Princeton, NJ: Princeton University Press.

Ehrenberg, D.B. (1974). The Intimate Edge in Therapeutic Relatedness. *Contemporary Psychoanalysis,* 10: 423–437.

Ferenczi, S. (1899). Spiritism, in *The Psychoanalytic Review,* Fodor, N. (trans.), (1963), 50A: 139–144.

———— (1915). Psychogenic anomalies of the vocal system. *International Journal of Psychoanalysis,* 3 (1): 25–28.

———— (1932). *The Clinical Diary of Sandor Ferenczi,* Dupont, J. (ed.), Balint, M. and Jackson, N.Z. (trans.), (1988), Cambridge, MA: Harvard University Press.

———— (1933). Freud's influence on medicine, in Ferenczi, S. (1952). *Final Contribution to the Problems and Methods of Psychoanalysis,* London: Hogarth, 143–155.

———— & Groddeck, G. (2002). *Sandor Ferenczi—Georg Groddeck Correspondence: 1921–1922.* Fortune, C. (ed.) London: Open Gate Press.

———— & Rank, O. (1924). *The Development of Psychoanalysis,* New York: Nervous and Mental Disease Publishing Company.

Ferro, A., Basile R. (2009). *The analytic field: A clinical concept,* London: Karnac.

Fortune, C. (2002). Georg Groddeck's influence on Sandor Ferenczi's clinical practice as reflected in their correspondence 1921–1933. *Psychoanalysis and History,* 4(1): 85–94.

Freud, S. (1912). Recommendations to physicians practicing psychoanalysis. *Standard Edition,* 1958: 12, 109–120, London: Hogarth Press.

———— (1915). The unconscious. *Standard Edition,* 1958. 14: 166–215, London: Hogarth Press.

———— (1923). The ego and the id. *Standard Edition,* 1958. 19: 1–66, London: Hogarth Press.

———— (1937). Constructions in Analysis. *The Standard Edition,* 1958, 23: 255–270, London: Hogarth Press.

———— & Ferenczi, S. (1993). *The Correspondence of Sigmund Freud and Sandor Ferenczi,* Vol. 1 (1908–1914), Brabant, E., Falzeder, E., Giampieri-Deutsch, P., eds., Hoffer, P. trans., Cambridge, MA: Belknap.

Galatzer-Levy, R.M. (2009). Good Vibrations: Analytic Process as Coupled Oscillations. *International Journal of Psychoanalysis,* 90(5): 983–1007.

Grinberg, L. (1956). Projective Counter-identification. *Review Psicoanálitica,* 13 (4): 507–511.

Groddeck, G. (1923). *The Book of the It,* London: Vision Press, 1950.

———— (1977). Schacht, L. (ed.), *The Meaning of Illness: Selected Psychoanalytic Writings by Georg Groddeck,* New York: International Universities Press.

Harris, A. and Kuchuck, S. (eds.), (2015). *The Legacy of Sandor Ferenczi,* London: Routledge.

Haynal, A. (2018). Mutuality. *American Journal of Psychoanalysis,* 78 (4): 342–349.

Hegel, G.W. F. (1949). *The Phenomenology of Mind*. Ballie, J.B. (trans.), New York: The MacMillan Company.

Heimann, P. (1950). On Counter-Transference. *International Journal of Psychoanalysis,* 31: 81–84.

Hoffer, P. (2008). Ferenczi's collaboration with Rank: On paradigm shift and the origins of complementarity in psychoanalysis. *American Journal of Psychoanalysis,* 68 (2): 129–138.

House, J. (2017). The ongoing rediscovery of *apres-coup* as a central Freudian concept. *Journal of the American Psychoanalytic Association,* 65 (5): 773–798.

Hristeva, G. (2019) "Primordial Chant". Sándor Ferenczi as an Orphic Poet. *American Journal of Psychoanalysis,* 79: 517–539.

Jacobs, T.J. (1986). On countertransference enactment. *Journal of the American Psychoanalytic Association,* 34: 289–307.

James, W. (1910). A suggestion about mysticism. *The Journal of Philosophy Psychology and Scientific Methods,* VII (4), February 17, 1910, 85–92.

Kirshner, L. 2017). *Intersubjectivity in Psychoanalysis,* London: Routledge.

Krauss, R.E. and Derrida, J. (1980). The law of genre, *Glyph* 7 in Chaplin, S. (2004). *Law, Sensibility, and the Sublime in Eighteenth-Century Women's Fiction: Speaking of Dread,* Farnum, UK: Ashgate Press. https://books.google.com/books?id=zOqNqq4i2ioC&pg=PA23

Lacan, J. (1977). The function and field of speech and language in psychoanalysis. in *Ecrits—A Selection.* Sheridan, A. (trans.), New York: Norton.

Laing, R.D. (1961). *Self and Others,* New York: Pantheon Books, 1969.

Lothane, Z. (1981–82). Listening with the third ear as an instrument in psychoanalysis: the contributions of Reik and Isakower. *Psychoanalytic Review,* 68: 487–504.

———— (1997). Freud and the Interpersonal. *International Forum of Psychoanalysis*, 6(3): 175–183.

———— (2009). Dramatology in Life, Disorder, and Psychoanalytic Therapy: A Further Contribution to Interpersonal Psychoanalysis. *International Forum of Psychoanalysis*, 18 (3): 135–148.

Mahler, M., Mahler, S., Pine, M.M., F., Bergman, A. (1973). *The Psychological Birth of the Human Infant*, New York: Basic Books.

Merleau-Ponty, M. (1968). *The Visible and the Invisible,* Evanston, IL: Northwestern University Press.

Mitchell, J. (1967). Lyrics to *Both Sides Now.* https://genius.com/Joni-mitchell-both-sides-now-lyrics

Ogden, T.H. (1994). The analytic third: Working with intersubjective clinical facts. *The International Journal of Psychoanalysis*, 75: 3–19.

Poster, M.F. (1997). An Hypothesis: The historical derivation of Freud's structural model of the mind. *Journal of Clinical Psychoanalysis,* 6 (2): 279–283.

———— (2009). Ferenczi and Groddeck: Simpatico—Roots of a Paradigm Shift in Psychoanalysis, *American Journal of Psychoanalysis,* 69: 195–206.

Poster, M.F., Hristeva, G., and Giefer, M. (2016). Georg Groddeck: "The pinch of pepper" of psychoanalysis, *American Journal of Psychoanalysis,* 69: 195–206.

Racker, H. (1953). A Contribution to the Problem of Counter-Transference. International Journal of Psychoanalysis, 34: 313–324.

Reik, T. (1949). *Listening with the Third Ear*, New York: Farrar, Straus and Company.

Renik, O. (2004). Intersubjectivity in psychoanalysis. *International Journal of Psychoanalysis*, 85(5): 1053–1056.

Rudnytsky, P.L. (2002). *Reading Psychoanalysis*, Ithaca, NY: Cornell University Press.

_____ (2022). *Mutual Analysis: Ferenczi, Severn, and the Origins of Trauma Theory*, London and New York: Routledge.

Sandler, J. (1976). Countertransference and Role-Responsiveness. *International Review of Psychoanalysis*, 3: 43–47.

Shedler, J. (2015). Where is the evidence for "evidence-based" therapy? *Journal of Psychological Therapies in Primary Care*, 4: 47–59.

Stern, D. (1985). *The Interpersonal World of the Infant*, New York: Basic Books.

Sullivan, H.S. (1953). *The Interpersonal Theory of Psychiatry*, Perry, H.S. and Gawel, M.L. (eds.), New York: Norton.

Thompson, M.G. (2005). Phenomenology of intersubjectivity: A historical overview of the concept and its clinical implications, in Mills, J. (ed.), *Relational Theory in Psychoanalysis*, Hillsdale, NJ: Jason Aronson.

Winnicott, DW. (1969). The use of an object, *International Journal of Psychoanalysis*, 50: 711–716.

An earlier version of this paper was presented at the 13th International Sandor Ferenczi Conference in Florence, Italy, May 4, 2018.

An earlier version of this paper appeared in *Capital Psychiatry*, Winter, 2025, Volume 6, Issue 1, pp. 17–21.

About the Contributors

Jon G. Allen, Ph.D., holds the position of Clinical Professor as a member of the Voluntary Faculty in the Department of Psychiatry and Behavioral Sciences at the Baylor College of Medicine. He is a member of the honorary faculty at the Houston Center for Psychoanalytic Studies and the adjunct faculty of the Institute for Spirituality and Health at the Texas Medical Center. He retired from clinical practice as a senior staff psychologist after 40 years at The Menninger Clinic, where he taught and supervised fellows and residents; conducted psychotherapy, diagnostic consultations, and psychoeducational programs; and led research on clinical outcomes. He continues to teach, write, and consult. His books include *Trusting in Psychotherapy, Restoring Mentalizing in Attachment Relationships: Treating Trauma with Plain Old Therapy, Mentalizing in Clinical Practice* (with Peter Fonagy and Anthony Bateman), *Coping with Trauma: From Self-Understanding to Hope,* and *Coping with Depression: From Catch-22 to Hope,* all published by American Psychiatric Association Publishing. Additional books are *Mentalizing in the Development and Treatment of Attachment Trauma* (Karnac) and *Traumatic Relationships and Serious Mental Disorders* (Wiley).

Daniel S. Benveniste, Ph.D., is a clinical psychologist with a private practice in Sammamish, Washington, near Seattle. He is a Visiting Professor of Clinical Psychology at the Wuhan Mental Health Center, in the People's Republic of China and an Honorary Member of the American Psychoanalytic Association. He is the author of *Libido, Culture, and Consciousness: Revisiting Freud's Totem and*

Taboo (2022), *The Interwoven Lives of Sigmund, Anna, and W. Ernest Freud: Three Generations of Psychoanalysis* (2015) and *The Venezuelan Revolution: A Critique from the Left* (2015). He is also the editor of *Anna Freud in the Hampstead Clinic: Letters to Humberto Nágera* (2015). He earned his BA (1976), MS (1979) and PhD (1990) in clinical psychology in the San Francisco Bay Area and was in supervision with Nathan Adler, Ph.D., for five years. He began his private practice and teaching career in San Francisco. From 1999 to 2010, he lived and worked in Caracas, Venezuela, where he maintained a private practice and taught psychotherapy at two universities. In 2010 he relocated to the Pacific Northwest with his wife, Adriana Prengler, FIPA.

David E. Cooper, Ph.D., is a psychoanalyst in private practice in Chevy Chase, Maryland. Dr. Cooper got his B.A. in Philosophy from Yale University and his Ph.D. in Clinical Psychology from George Washington University. He did his psychoanalytic training at the Washington Psychoanalytic Institute (now the Washington Baltimore Institute), where he has been on the faculty for many years. He is past president of the Washington Center for Psychoanalysis and past founder and co-chair of the Center's Diversities Committee. He is Clinical Professor of Psychiatry at the George Washington University School of Medicine. In the 90's he was at Chestnut Lodge Hospital, where he founded and directed a day hospital program for severe personality disorders.

J. Todd Dean, M.D., is a psychiatrist and psychoanalyst in private practice in St. Louis, MO. He is currently the director of education at the St. Louis Psychoanalytic Institute, and has been on the editorial boards of *JAPA* and *Division/Review*. He is also a member of the Association for Psychotherapy and Psychoanalysis in Ireland. He has had

various publications, mostly book reviews and brief essays, in *Division/Review, JAPA* and *The American Journal of Psychoanalytic Psychology.*

Lance Dodes, M.D., is a Training and Supervising Analyst Emeritus at the Boston Psychoanalytic Society and Institute, member of the faculty of the New Center for Psychoanalysis (Los Angeles) and retired assistant clinical professor of psychiatry at Harvard Medical School. He is the author of many journal articles and book chapters and three books about understanding the psychology of addiction as a compulsive behavior. Dr. Dodes has been honored by the Division on Addictions at Harvard Medical School for "Distinguished Contribution" to the study and treatment of addictive behavior and has been elected a Distinguished Fellow of the American Academy of Addiction Psychiatry. He is an Associate Editor of the *Journal of the American Psychoanalytic Association.* He contributed the chapter "Sociopathy" to the recent bestselling book, *The Dangerous Case of Donald Trump.*

Fred Gioia, M.D., is a board-certified adult psychiatrist and psychoanalyst based in Dallas, Texas. He is a clinical instructor in the Department of Psychiatry at UT Southwestern Medical Center and maintains a private practice specializing in psychoanalytic psychotherapy and psycho-pharmacology, including ketamine-assisted psychotherapy. He currently serves as Curriculum Chair for the Dallas Psychoanalytic Center and leads the Workshop Series for the American Psychoanalytic Association's Committee on Artificial Intelligence. He received his medical degree from Texas A&M Health Science Center and completed his residency in psychiatry at UT Southwestern. Dr. Gioia also holds a master's degree in applied cognition

and neuroscience from the University of Texas at Dallas and completed his psychoanalytic training at the Dallas Psychoanalytic Center.

Jane S. Hall, LCSW, FIPA, former President of the Contemporary Freudian Society, past boards of the IPA, ApsaA, member AAPCSW. National and international lecturer; author of: *The Power of Connection (2022)* IPBooks; *Roadblocks on the Journey of Psychotherapy* (2004) and *Deepening the Treatment* (1998), published by Jason Aronson; and other articles. On faculties of three NY institutes in the US and China. Member of the Tampa Bay Institute. Founder of the New York School for Psychoanalytic Psychotherapy and Psychoanalysis, Jane created and was the first director of the Psychotherapy Track at CFS. A graduate of the Institute for the Study of Psychotherapy, and the Contemporary Freudian Society-Institute, she speaks, teaches and consults nationally and internationally specializing in small group and individual supervision via Zoom.

M. Sagman Kayatekin, M.D., graduated from Hacettepe University Medical Faculty and completed residency trainings in adult psychiatry at Hacettepe and Medical College of Wisconsin. He had a four-year fellowship at the Austen Riggs Center and graduated from Boston Psychoanalytic Society and Institute as an adult psychoanalyst. He was faculty at Hacettepe, UMass, and Baylor. He is currently faculty and former President of the Board at Center for Psychoanalytic Studies, Visiting Professor at Tongji Medical College, China. He also has faculty position at Psychoanalytic Institute for Central Asia, Kazakhstan. In the last 40 years, he maintained a dual interest in clinical care and teaching while directing various clinical organizations. He taught, published and presented in a wide range

of national and international forums. His most recent role was as the Medical Director of Professionals Program at the Menninger Clinic. All through these years he also had a small private practice on the sides. Since 2022, he mainly works in his private practice and is involved in clinical work, teaching, lecturing, writing and supervision. Some of his current areas of interest are pedagogy of psychoanalytic training, ego capacities of the mind, the central role of language in understanding the mind, and the controversial/creative subjects in psychoanalytic theory and practice.

Luba Kessler, M.D. is a psychiatrist trained in classical psychoanalysis, practicing in Long island City, New York. Among influences on her professional thought, practice, teaching and writing are: demographic and linguistic multiculturalism spanning life from the Soviet sphere to the diversity of America; interest in sociopolitical geography/ history and study of Freudian metapsychology and neuropsychoanalysis. All have combined into a concentric view of psychological life of body/psyche in the surround of family, community, society, and culture at large.

Rona Knight, Ph.D., is one of the seminal thinkers and researchers in the domain of development in psychoanalysis. Dr. Knight's groundbreaking longitudinal study on children's psychic development during middle childhood (*PSC* 2005, 2011) demonstrated that concepts like nonlinear development and dynamic systems theory offer a more effective framework for understanding development than traditional psychoanalytic theories. Dr. Knight is a child, adolescent and adult psychoanalyst; assistant professor of psychiatry and pediatrics at Boston University School of Medicine; and a faculty member and child supervisor at BPSI. She is on the board of the Anna Freud Foundation and on the editorial board of

JAPA. She is a Senior Editor of the Psychoanalytic Study of the Child. Dr. Knight has published and presented papers on child development, nonlinear dynamic systems theory, gender and clinical child psychoanalysis. In 2003 she won the Albert Solnit Award for her *PSC* paper on narrative building in child psychoanalysis.

David Lichtenstein, Ph.D. is a psychoanalyst in private practice in NYC. He is a Faculty and Board Member of Pulsion Institute, NY, and a Faculty Member at the NYU Post Doc. Institute for Psychoanalysis and Psychotherapy, IPTAR, PINC, and the CUNY Doctoral Program in Clinical Psychology. He is co-editor of the recent book *The Lacan Tradition* (Routledge, 2018) and teaches an independent course entitled *The Clinical Implications of the Work of Jacques Lacan.* He was the Founding Editor of *DIVISION/ Review: A Quarterly Psychoanalytic Forum*, a Co-Founder of *Après-Coup* Psychoanalytic Association, and a participant at *Das Unbehagen.*

Mark F. Poster, M.D., is a graduate of the University of Pennsylvania and its medical school. During that time, he spent a year at University College London and a summer at The Neurologic Institute at Queen Square. He then trained in internal medicine, medical oncology, and psychiatry, all at Tufts Medical Center. During that time, he was a senior medical resident at Boston City Hospital. His psychoanalytic training was at the Psychoanalytic Institute of New England, East (PINE). Dr. Poster served for 50 years at the Boston Veterans Administration Healthcare System, first on the medical staff at Jamaica Plain, and then on the psychiatry staff at Brockton. He also served for 5 years as director of geriatric psychiatry at Charles River Hospital in Wellesley, MA and for 12 years as psychiatric consultant at Campion

Center, a Jesuit residence, in Weston, MA. He had a private practice in West Newton, MA for 58 years. Dr. Poster's main interests have been medical history, mind/body relationships, trauma, psychotherapy integration, and recovery. His publications include the biography of Georg Groddeck, a German physician and pioneer of psychosomatic medicine; the friendship between Groddeck and Sandor Ferenczi, a pioneer of psychoanalysis; thoughts on war; psychotherapy integration, including the introduction of the "shaving brush model". Dr. Poster had teaching appointments at Harvard Medical School (Assistant Professor) and Boston University Medical School (Instructor) while teaching psychiatry residents at the Brockton VA for 45 years. Now retired from clinical practice, Dr. Poster teaches Fellows at the PINE Psychoanalytic Society of New England and serves on the editorial boards of several psychoanalytic journals.

Francisco Somarriva Pinto, MSW, MSc, is a Chilean psychoanalyst and licensed clinical social worker. He works at the Outpatient Psychiatry Department of Cambridge Health Alliance in Boston and in private practice. He received the professional title of psychologist from Pontificia Universidad Católica de Chile and his MSc in Theoretical Psychoanalytic Studies from University College London, United Kingdom. Then, he underwent his psychoanalytic training at the Institute of the Chilean Psychoanalytic Association and is an associated member of that society. Mr. Somarriva has also collaborated in different roles for Psychoanalytic Electronic Publishing—PEP-Web, and was a member of the IPA Communications Committee while being a psychoanalyst-in-training. Finally, he is the Volume 6 co-editor and Glossary editor of *The Complete Works of Donald W. Winnicott* translation into Spanish.

www.ingramcontent.com/pod-product-compliance
Lightning Source LLC
Chambersburg PA
CBHW060228030426
42335CB00014B/1368